T0328359

White Masks

White Masks

Ebi Yeibo

malthouse ⋊𝓅

Malthouse Press Limited

Lagos, Benin, Ibadan, Jos,Port-Harcourt, Zaria

© Ebi Yeibo 2019
First Published 2019
ISBN: 978-978-56690-7-7

Published and manufactured in Nigeria by

Malthouse Press Limited
43 Onitana Street, Off Stadium Hotel Road,
Off Western Avenue, Lagos Mainland
E-mail: malthouselagos@gmail.com
Tel: +234 802 600 3203

Distributors
African Books Collective Ltd
Email: abc@africanbookscollective.com
Website: http://www.africanbookscollective.com

For Emilia Mami,
For the love and prayers...

Acknowledgements

I am eternally indebted to Professor Hyginus Ekwuazi, for the kind heart and humility; and to Professors Sunday Awhefeada and Ogaga Okuyade, for the abiding support and encouragement. God bless you abundantly.

But every day wears a sword
beneath its white-laced drapes.

Tanure Ojaide

Your colour is camouflage and bait, whitened castle-
hiding the eternal stench from your stinking entrails.

Oyeniyi Okunoye

Foreword

The [white] masks of this poetry collection—what do they portend?

That, indeed, is the question at the beating heart of this anthology. For that is the insistent question which the poet deftly slices and dices into a thousand and one intriguing pieces—flung and scattered in poem after poem.

Early enough, we encounter it—what Eliot would term: the objective correlative:

> ...a white mask
> Covering a gruelling monster in human blood
> Plodding fulsome flags in faltering winds.

And from the moment we encounter it, this motif, there is no difficulty in following it all through the highways and byways where words and images meet, collide and scatter in different directions. That the reader does manage to keep this white mask in focus is simply on account of this: that all the various elements of this entire collection have been made to morph into a single unifying idea.

Note that these highways and byways along which words and imagery trail each other, hold hands with each other and walk opposite each other—these highways and byways all have this in common: not just the various glimpses of this white mask, this monster, these fulsome flags, this wind in which the flags flutter and, of course, this land in which it all takes place: all this is not the sum total of what they have in common. For me, what is even more significant, is that at any point on this highway and this byway, any backward look on travelled roads is in effect a new gaze forward.

It has since become commonplace, the awareness that nuanced into every work of art is the argument for how that work should be read. I have always believed that this 'how' can in no way be disconnected from the role scripted for the reader/social actor in relation to the work. Yes, the reader/social actor inevitably defined by his/her social value systems and life experiences. In this connection, what I do find here is that the poet has scripted many roles for the reader, for the social actor—as an extra, a witness, a victim, an accomplice or a distant passer-by. I suppose each reader has to pick his role.

Ebi Yeibo's *White Masks* is a collection inspired by hope. In whichever way it is read, it cannot but invite a political and social argument.

Highly recommended to the discerning reader—to anyone who takes more than a passing interest in any aspect of modern Nigerian poetry.

Professor Hyginus Ekwuazi
University of Ibadan

The Poems

OF MASKS AND WHIRLWINDS

I

On the doorway to the plenitude
The mass servers enact, with abstinence
And throbbing rosaries, a patriot pees
Ascends to the mountaintop, on iron winds

The soul robust with blood and bone
Needs cleansing in draughty sunlight;
A dissonant priest fronting an evanescent smile,
In secret prayers for downright odd stuff,

Or offside conventional stuff,
On the throng angling for terrestrial colours,
Needs penitence in a whorl of white light,
Like a prodigal pawing the wind

In the wilderness, for a long lost inheritance;
The cricket makes strident melody
In awry holes and twilight, serenading open seascapes
A shrieking unrest marks a lunatic's freedom

From the devil's uncircumcised phallus
Which, they say, is unmanageable,
Like a failed break, or a virus-ravaged handset
Swells with the rains, like a river;

A litany of questions crowd the head
To release pent-up fancies and fire;
Comb improbable spots for the node
Morphing into masks and whirlwinds...

II
A lambent chorus revels in stale songs
Fondles cracked souls in the ripening sun
Beyond the soprano between lurid laps
Dainty petal of clay, high on aphrodisiac

Beyond the winking memorials of silhouettes
Prowling in the middle of River Forcados
Pouring bacchanalian jibes on moonglow
Gathering steam on the sly sweetness of piassava

A monstrous tyrant holds the rains
From the cosy confines of his closet, barring talkative thunder
And the howling sky goes to sleep, perfunctorily,
Like growling Bingo enjoying intimate strokes on the head

Who courts a harridan with martial song?
The heated soul ferments in the embers of memory
Recounts the quandary of the village healer
Over bumps in the bloodstream

Drought drowns the soul in a torrid orchestra
No surcease in sight!
This earth is burdened
By butts and crumbling banisters.

III
Bruised cannons flourish in forgotten fringes,
Defiled street corners; lewd interspaces
Suffused in some sweet-smelling incense
In moonmist; the imprint of grey scriptures

Clings to the sun, vending false wares
In half-light; empty shells and catacombs,
Sometimes, containing ash and water
More noxious than faeces on the altar

A masterpiece sprouts from a bankrupt carnival
Scattered locusts on green herbage at the riverside
Produce whirlwinds in the soul; scraps of earth
Muscle their way to the moon, then downward strides

To dry land, following one naughty beacon
In mundane wavelashes; on the pathway
Behind the sacred woods, serenading the gods
A muffled melody in the belly of a scabbard.

An abundance of fingered dreams in the air
Naked pincers prowl the plains of Sambisa[1]
Speaking of a thousand raptures
Running waters and galloping antelopes.

This world remains burdened by its own ascent
Sometimes, stretchered in open tremors
The bubble bursts in tangled compromises
Gasping for breath at the feet of Odele[2]

Burdened by its own caprices and gashes
Wayward consciences carried by a lamb's face;
Countless paunches from the commonwealth
Foil the shrill sound of crickets on Bomadi beach.

IV
Always, breath rides on precipices unto fable
Light, without spunk or hymen,
Inhabits the world's end, awaiting impregnation

The caterpillar perforates the greenery of blood
Throwing a juicy world into gangrenous whirlwinds
A disconsolate dance on boulders, without name or pattern

---

[1] Boko Haram fortress, Borno State, Nigeria.
[2] A god at Ayakoromo.

I hear footfalls echoing in the brothel
At Bomadi market waterside[3] when the sun goes down
Shadows on queue await dour wages in heavenly holes

The tinctured aura is encased in broad hips
Beyond blood knots, beyond frisking
Beyond tingling monuments dispersed in primal folds

Always, a wild soldier prowls in the pants
To reconstruct a bridge broken halfway
In the depths at midtown at twilight

Muezzins gambol round the borders as *madibas*
Wheezing in the early morning breeze
Hoisting husks and hebetude

They revel in a sandhouse, like a toddler;
Dew-draped greenery to a graveyard
Sprouting sore tales in the streets.

V
Pilgrims bask in wiry faiths; flaunting stakes
On marshy ground; and argonauts stand on waves,
Wheedling fate spread out in the sun

Breeding fallow footnotes, staid bouquets,
Buried without a sepulchre, in tawdry toil
A clear maze, a warped promenade

Abiding relics of a freaky fair in the wind
Slimy memory; headlamp of pathfinders – spotlighting
Swimming ducklings in River Forcados at dawn

---

[3] A brothel owned by late Chief Tekeme, better known as "Teks."

Call it the parasoled path in man-made deserts
Who else travels this forest at midnight?
Who else revels in this painted orgasm?

A moping mascot plays with waterlilies
In flow tide; limp leopards lap water to their fill
Gossamer of unforgettable years in the countryside.

NAKED SEASCAPES

I

A suppliant silence stills the flutter
Of *Agbaya bou;*[*] though the embers glow unseen
Sprouting eerie gushes and cringing impulses;

The tiro's lot in the klieg lights –
Intonation and a gliding voice
Are never conclusive in a piece of theatre.

I always remember grandma's words
To an elder cousin on a conjugal journey
In a deliberate, deep-throated voice

As if heeding the inherent insight
Erased the gathering clouds up there
The fierce lightning and thunder:

Take with you wholesome gifts
From the river's bounties, to open the road;
This virgin seems implacable and unbendable.

Harpy tendons of memory, flailing pranks
In birdsong, by the riverside full of dead things
Fanning triumphant fates on quicksand.

The chimeras fallen, like a stroke patient,
The inviolable mesh of maggots meander
In monstrous monotony, fondling pointed nipples

---

[*] A mystical forest at Ndoro, Bayelsa State.

Hidden in highway briefcases and night gowns
Ready for flight in half-darkness, in the bristling traffic.
Who would not clasp the dizzying statuette

Of a living blonde at Abraka library hosting
A demurring fruitage on the altar – a chaliced vault,
A leprous slew, to stoke the fire fallowing in the blood?

II

Here to the painted bonds, covert harmonies
The acidulous touch of living Mona Lisa
Spreading corncobs with scattered teeth
In the skein of crescent meadows
The slothful clotting of halcyon days

The sundered tremolo by the heavenly choir
The desolate ferment, foreclosed before birth
In naked seascapes; obdurate birds
Flutter in the wind, deserting their own song
In the middle of nowhere, seeking succour in unknown seas.

Here to the broken anchorage on a cockpit
At the crucial moment, whirling up recondite blood
The burgeoning star barred from the sea
The crocodile slit open in public glare
The odorous entrails a choleric memorabilia.

Wanton bulbuls howl at the knotted wind
Above the smudged waters, demurely flowing
On infinitude's lap, beyond the prism of punctuation,
Importunate and swollen, in effervescent laughter
Under sullen skies, delineated manacles.

THE PRIEST'S POUCH

The wreathed crowd at the sacred water front,
Like the stalked moon far away,
Jumps over snares scattered
In the wind, the phantom phosphorescence

In towering summits
The fleecing blossom-
The bombax flowers in the dry season,
Foreshadowing greenery.

Hurrah to the red strand in the priest's pouch
Always awake with unheard footsteps
Rankles the bones with snug solicitude
Scans the whirlpool for the keyword to life

Ingrafted in globules of slime and grime
Along splintered harmonies, inconstant
Diabolical crystals; a scurrilous flame
Lights up breasts of hidden monuments.

Never mind a river mongrel roaming
The landscape, revelling in the sacrament
Of smoke or gunpowder, or some sore pastime
In the name of survival which, itself,

Is much maligned in the spirit
Some credulous self-delusion, a white mask
Covering a gruelling monster in human blood
Plodding fulsome flags in faltering winds.

But how can one purify the wind
With a welter of ballistic fart?
Silence is a tough call in these climes
Pummelled by priests' crimson pranks.

I have seen them touch the throbbing earth
Then their tongues with naked fingers
Swearing with the name of the God of hosts
To uphold the heritage with gleeful sanctity

Derailing without contrition before the first cockcrow;
The immeasurable latitude of open chattels
Squandering impeccable stars in synthetic thraldom
The unpurged patrimony of waste and quicklime;

The battle of shadows burgeons into myth
You cannot slash or stem or mow down
A stony memory replete with living rodents
A market without motion, disclaiming

The heart's placid waters, interposed
With the salt-sweetness of sea breeze
Crackling transcendental things borne in knots
Of black hair, viding growth and vainglory.

The lunatic splendour of a prodigal
Carrying the scarab's callused coarseness
On his shoulders, drifting underground –
A cascade of colourless caverns on mountain tops.

The slovenly dust; memory of harmattan winds
The mounting desire for a sea ride
Seeing the rampaging waves and whales
Horsemen and fluttered egos in bruised little worlds

The disconsolate voice crying about moonmarks
The junk cocktails and biting budgets in monochrome
The synthetic carrions full of niggling flies
The teetering vacuities of simulated abundance.

PAGAN DELUSION

Homecoming is a far-fetched farewell
An owl's shriek, in distant woods
Bearing no summons or telltale signals.

A burst of phantom lights
Proclaiming unction with ethereal fanfare
In a glasshouse; stripped of the luxury
Of insulation – the votary of flowing streams

Where all the curses spewed in coven intersect;
Putrescent juice interspersed with sanguine cobwebs
Consanguinity bars a probe with binoculars
Howling at dogs baying at the moon!

Needless mumbling about marbles
In dusky winds and phantoms
Abhorrent pillars pricking penance and lent
Showing off proportionate accouchement

Needless uncoupling memory in a plenum
Of crooked paths; a rowdy whorl of shadows
The bristling warfare of the soul
The legion backwaters and transience

The lumbering notaries and staircases
Leading to nowhere; the turbid tunnels
And footfalls and eyelashes, like
A twisted kiss on an odorous belle

The inviolable trickery; overflowing gulch
In blossoming heartbeats, fingers duteously
Roving in breathing sacred groves
Behind closed doorways, in whirling blood

In star-filled nights; the plutonic freshness
Hollow expendable trappings of pontifical gestures,
Like butterflies exuding manifold colours
Of terrestrial dust; the formic acid of pismire

Surpasses the lure of semen, even in the drizzling dawn –
A loveliness luminous and voluptuous
Dream teaser, suckles the tactile blood,
In drift; a surfeit of invisible stones

In conflating counterpoise; calculative clowns
On juicy peaks, without rungs
Proactive spendthrifts, poaching the wind
Like a buzzard savouring luxuriant prey.

The arcana of wiles in the cathedral
The bouquets of episcopal carnation
Showy junk in delirious underbrush.

NOTHING

No catacombs, no sacred groves, no desecration in the wind,
Even in the tallest of drifts; no throaty laughters
In the hearth; no desiccation in the shrubbery of the soul;

Only the echoes of tidal waves in Ageh[*]
In the dead of night, where fishermen no longer flower
In their sweat; struggling with crude knots.

No unflinching footfalls, no unction
Of droning night rain on village thatches;
There is a tentative submerging of triumph,

Of vagrant souls; delirious blood routs the headstrong
With lightning on the highway; a plumed prison
Where innocence is faeces, an exulted guilt...

This space stands on its head; a mounting filth
In the spirit, raucous silences containing bile, a syllable
Of sullen contours drowned in the countless stars

Illumining the world; a nocturnal transparency, steamy rains
Breeding sweat; an outer peace laden with inner crisis,
A pregnant compunction; loves full of flea

Resident outside the tapestry of the heart
In some dark corner of the stony street
Undermining the infinitude of God's grace –

A bawling burden to dance without drumbeats
Self-imposed, a blundering virtuoso in a burst
Of debouching, remembering one's halcyon roots.

---

[*] A riverine community.

No quintessence of ancient delectation.
No whistling name full of fancy, no galloping presence,
Even in customary self-effacement;

Soft stones litter the wind, callused waters flow through veins
In a benighted and desolate house in the grove
Quickens hollow spirits; kneads the nakedness

And discord into a conjugal masterpiece
The manual of beauty hidden in metallurgical gullies
And pits; the soul collapses in a compromise

There is no one to mend the fence (which is not propitious)
Cobble the coastland in a patrimony of iron-cast ribbons
Upturn the blistering smog in the foliage

The calcified emptiness, hollow hills
Solicitous, as if there is a difference between
Being buried in ash or flying

In caked clouds, with wet wings; man
Is a gathering of water and bone; a pyramid
Of husks and perfumes; an altar of nothing

At twilight; not even broken bits and butts
Or shadows or side shows – nothing; ultimately nothing;
This is the drift in the lengthening domino

The flowering and triumph; the winking eyes
The immaculate thighs man buries his head
In his ruinous unremembering in the sun.

THIS DYING SONG

White streaks mellow down the wind's strides
On the dew-drenched path to the river nun
Carrying droves of flailing incubus in their trail

Plaintive cadences, the hues of webs, caked routes
Knotty stumps, serrated palms, cragged crevices
All soak up the soothing rays of the sun

Like sponge soapy fluid, like an unpurged stomach
After a heavy meal of *Kekefiyai* at Mama Boye[*]
And the surrounding homesteads wear worsted brows

Lose their spine, glazed in avoidable self-abnegation
Entrapped in their own rusty glow, in broad daylight –
A drunken star caught up in darkly sidewalls.

An adventurous dandy jumps over living tunnels
With a bent tongue; the lure
Of mountain tops recedes in twilight, even

In soldierly hearts, planted on sloppy path
To stoke faggots of this dying song
The accompanying gong singeing the sweet rhythm

In the middle of the sea, leaving the famished blood
Floating in the wind; in some sizzling climes,
Smoke rises from forests without trackable fire

The storm that brews in an old woman's waist
The range as wild as young blood on the highway
Is never hard to contain; steady, mild plunges

---

[*] A popular restaurant in Yenagoa.

Plants the moon in the moon in tickling weather
Though on show is a monument of wide-awake years
Through patches of long, convoluted clouds.

No rhetoric, however burnished with courtesy
Or guile, or sophistry, fills up an empty stomach
When the head turns in a non-existent whirlwind

Or drowns in the brackish promise of tides
The blooming dam of dissimulators
Seeding noontide dreams, sacraments of wind players.

The humdrum dust sentinels the doorway of desire
Wracking the tender body of the universe
Like scriptures diverted to a decrepit end;

Cadences clothed in a haunting cortege
The contagion of crusted curses, the bazaar of puddles,
All soil the bounties of the road.

The labyrinthine attic that is home
The chattering shadows, the sanctity
Of a pigeon's coo, a pageant of simulated blizzards

Posing as spectral beacons; unheard songs
Soothe primal sores, the somnolent enchantment
Of estranged melodies, epigraph of a belaboured hiccup

As reprehensible as a forgotten munitions dump
A lady's white cloth after a wild night
A spool of rivulets littered with faeces

A smudged make-up on Christmas,
Raped fragrances steeped
In the stillness of blood; a blaze

Reported in an Indian firecracker shop,
Taking in its trail seven succulent souls,
Even with sinewy barricades

And curfews; phantom suns illuminate
Winding phalanxes, a blooming cellar,
Smelly fingers of an itchy anus

All finely poised in a sweet night without sweat,
Spelling unavowed strands of a common creed
Mustering earthy glory in gory thoughts

The droning voice in the silence of the sea
The harbour flashes red lights
In the middle of the night, pregnant.

LOVELY BITS OF WIND

The enclosing green shrubs, far away
From locusts and caterpillars – their melancholy
Blossoms in the hobbling waves; golden mornings
In combat, scraps of distant rainbows that catch the eye

Where nights, once triumphant, like Kenibra-owei[+]
Who threw the mystical short man with standing dreadlocks
That blocked the solitary bush path at Amassoma
Challenging every wayfarer to a wrestling bout

Are sallow and dour, like a sick goldfish
Panting in warm, homely tides, pandering
To parched bits of wind, praying
Against the fisherman's ubiquitous net, hurrying

A withering world to the sore point
Of self-doubt; a lethal blight, like
Black pod disease on cocoa farms in Daada[*]
A castaway heaped out of flowing meadows

A silvery song hangs in a devout's throat
Sour homilies planted in loamy souls; I say again,
This earth needs a mop, not an effete broom
Rummaging in distant dumps, not

[+] Literally translated as "one-handed man". Legend has it that a long time ago, a mystical man claimed ownership of the Amassoma forest and insisted that only people who threw him in a wrestling bout could pass through. Nobody had achieved that feat. His victims fell sick and died in days. Unexpectedly, Kenibra-owei threw him not only once, but three good times. He came back home with an uncontrollable sense of triumph and became an instant legend.

[*] A cocoa producing community in Ondo State, Nigeria

The warped whistle blowing hot in pregnant winds
A surreal sacrament hovers over the earth
Squirts from pearly souls, atones for the fouled air

The indulgent lechery in the blood of brotherhood
The sail is taken out of a nation's cruise
The birdsong hangs on distant rafters

The soaring famine in the soul
The rank indifference, like a walking duck,
Spawns hidden daggers of night men,

Prodigals eavesdropping in withered raffia groves
Fragments of the shadow on the highway
Pulling through time's holy forge

To the foothill of dreams; the harried hinges
Thrill the soul, like eating soured soup
Full of saucy prawn in a dream

A cast-iron iconoclast, startled, sells ancient secrets
To luscious thighs of damsels, intermingling
With the apparition in the blood, dressed

In an archangel's earthy twines, the vale of bends
Surfing underground routes in solitary passage
Foreshadowing the sumptuous sapor tossed about

In tidal waves; ceaseless bends in the breasts,
Helplessly toiling, as a cockroach lying belly-up;
Foundering stars, bearing a funeral cloth

Fade into the clouds, the nude heavens,
A dimly aura all around open closures
Breathes on the crowd waiting for the word

Heavy iron-sheets on their heads
Trudging along the tedious road to the tuberous farm
A Babel of tracks leading to muddied streams

The thirst writ on the gale of still dust
Hanging in the wind, telegraphing the cobra curled,
Hiding in the thick groves at twilight.

PENANCE

The bulk of ghosts in sandhouse on the beach
Point accusative fingers at the sun
Oblivious of the caterpillars' headlong invasion

Of sacred groves, perforating medicinal herbage and myths.
On the hinges of reckoning, lovers court
Wanton grief, unheard by a third party,

That keeps them awake at midnight
A gust of dry things casts a living spell
On wet glands in the sky, baring

A putrescent weakness; delirious waters
Wait for heavenly unction to come down
To earth as newborns – glassed souls

Suckling on tender breasts; always,
Tangled bubbles float half-hearted
On the sea's surface, striding eternal on earth

With a diamond cross ordinary eyes do not see
Even in their blithesome ubiquitousness, like
The wild fires with an unforgettable damsel

On the arms of sensual blood and balm
The night before and the night before the night before
Lost in the delirious longing watching

Moaning shadows in the mist, through a keyhole
Delirious lavender, carrying fire and honey
In one breath, which overwhelms the priest

Dead in the faith; who can gloss over
The fireflies and the waves at noon
Clinging to desert skies without the rainbow?

Dreams of waterfall on parched waists
Hanging in dead groves; clamorous
In worsted catacombs; penance makes a man naked

With a covering of green leaves in moonlight;
Expectant, like a burdened pilgrim
On christ's footmarks; even the tortoise

Slips irredeemably in its black and white craft
Cutting a bat-infested tree against its own breath
Ascending to a zero-place, with imagined wings.

DEBTORS

Debtors find no repose in homely breath
Light rings an alarm bell among shadows
Among covens, stirring to halt newborns
Bruising the tender flesh of dawn

Beyond reproach; bruising the wind carrying
A garland of voices and variegated moods –
You can't farm a fruitful forest

With wrinkled hoes; you'd rather not
Smile at the outcome of tragedy and wreckage –
A worn-out heart lacks the power of ascent
Living cannons fade on the pulpit

Powered by facades
The snugness of a dream is a searing rhyme
On the moon; a man's loin a roadblock

In half-light, in the wake
Of shibboleths and birdsong
The rainbow itself can be smeared
With black charcoal

Or suffer a broken face in thunder
The congregation famishcs on weed-tanned altars
On the fringes of unseen rivers, or a canvas

Of clay hanging on an ancient rack
Where it is a taboo
To table your loins
For a white duel on a porch;

Decant your perspective and go home a freeborn
Without a scathing burn on your palms or tongue
There is a tremor in the void and the sapling

Bequeathed by a clairvoyant priest;
The warped clamour of heavenly wits
Never gathers steel in the battlefront
Even with stitches in green forests –

The monkey which strays into a net
In the air, in broad daylight
Is stripped of its stylized gifts on trees

Drained of its brains; the key
To an acrobatic wandering,
Without limitations or catalytic oil,
Displaying its ethereal essence in the wilderness,

Plucking up the bloom that sucks breath out
Of brothels, humped in some shrivelled street corner
Squarely saddled, after the toil, with some drift

In the wind, gasping for fresh notes without a blast
At sundown; fraudulent arguments that teach nothing
On flow tide; hollow gimmicks choke newborns to death;
The travailed soul walks on unyielding altars

With a prodded step of faith at the border
Waiting for the hangman's noose; like the Israelites,
Recovers all losses, after the stress on red seas.

TIME'S ESSENCE

This earth is luminous, without smoke or smog
Without artillery or combat or arcane footprints

Leading to waterfalls and sandhouses
Lean Cathedrals and dreamy congregations

Without bulbulous contraptions wracking the wind
Ash sprinkled on free-flowing streams

In the cover of night, in a festival of fireflies
The shadow posing as light's acolyte is raped

Caught in the net cast in empty space
Fishermen hem in flailing folks, declare

A meal with dead fish, the odour enchanting
And compulsive, emblazoned by time's essence

Which is the movement of man's mind to no destination
Pulverized beyond recognition, without a burial

Only a lengthening cloud hovering over shafts of light
Harbinger of ruination and death so common

In the sallow streets; the pubescence of uncharted holes
The abiding slur cast on blossoming fields

A doodling dandy knows how to seduce
Opposite blood, riding on illusion or delirium –

A village belle's bait, a villainous tenderness
Expands the coast, like a heathen miracle

Exacerbating the black knots in the wind
A faltering soul finds a straw from nowhere

Sometimes, solitude itself is a nudge (an awakening)
Raining in the soul in moments of phosphorescence

Embroiled in mermaids' prayer beads
A decrepit impulse to avoid shrouded things

Or husks partying in the wind; a projectile
Of dreams and rubbles when brothers

Stalk one another; breathing down gazelle necks
The sail of the soul hits a snag of blood.

Implosion has stripped herself on the bedside
A bullet or bomb or earthquake erupts in daylight

Rocking ancient bonds, sacred hinges across time
Stacked green groves lying fallow in esoteric lust

In the forest of ghosts, black gods
Always orchestrate a loud whisper

To heal the wind, muffling sensual songs
Hanging in memory, surging thoughts at crossroads

The roots of mahoganies are ripped with abandon
By gruelling quakes, begetting a cluster of yawning crevices

Where flowers sprout, panning for love in tiny rays, otherwise
Non-existent; love departed the world long ago in the garden.

In its stead, a pyramid of impure breath
Mingled with delirium; blood is hobbled

By flowery coups of any mould
Ancestral knots, scrawls of sighing souls

Entangled in a lost world, in shallow depths; a discomfiture,
A sweltering sweetness that touches the brain

Open verdure, coy in the wind, invisible to sages who probe
The powers nuzzling honeycombs, twisted contours

Crystalline faces, like an unhealing red sore
Inflicted from coven to filter the air, free endangered nostrils.

WHITE MASKS

I
Out of the swirling smoke, hosts of wholly
Grey imaginations, frigid sentiments, the bristling bile
Floating in the wind, springs a loveless sainthood.

No relief in sight in immaculate sand dunes
No respite in risping nights...
No missals of juice, over the years...

And dawn appears again as a newborn
With phosphorescent wrinkles and blood-shot eyes
Dyed in fragrant white masks –

Votaries of memory, limbers of a lurid landscape
Laden with laughter and shadows and heelless dreams
Consummate green and blisters and locusts in one space

Without a mustard hope of parting in the overcast skies
Breathing down necks of dancers in the wind
Countless dandies demur in the midday sun

Devolves knotted harmonies on marooned blood
Like the extended glow in coven
Where, they say, everyday is Christmas

Where, they say, iridescent spirits soar in hollow pouches
Spurred on by white bubbles in the sea
Slaying in the abandoned pew, in the censer

That covers the circumference of the altar, where
The alabaster sparkles infinitely, forgotten by faithfuls
Like some tiro medic his scalpel in the womb.

The shores remain naked in the sun
The white knots tangles of sin and light -
The wide pathways to scarified sanctuaries.

And, just last night, in a dream, I saw a snake;
Its head in a white basin, the rest of its languid body
On the floor, a dry brownish leaf in its mouth.

The end is far away, seemingly foreclosed
Buried beyond effacement or blushing
Beyond the throbbing war of blowing wind

Beyond the shadows wagging their tails
In moonlight, to welcome strangers suckling
On turgid void; this earth remains arcane;

No wonder, when an antelope struggles to safety
From a trap of barbed wire, by chance,
It runs four-forty from any semblance of a rope.

This earth remains an open anus
With teeming fart, bringing out water
To descant the wind that ignites

The whirlpool at Ofenibenghan,* seeking
Transcendence on patrimony's palms
Swaying dire waists, like sensuous *Owigiri*+ dancers

In the grip of Ebizimor's⁴ candid vibes
In endless wake-keeps in the creeks
The accompanying tangos anywhere, in half-light.

---

* A riverine community.
+ The dominant Ijaw highlife dance.
⁴ King Robert Ebizimor

I saw seven locked padlocks
Snuggling somewhere
In the depths of the river

Stalling motion in human affairs
O the hunter does not divulge
All he sees in the forest...

The river remains placid, with occasional ripples,
Though severely cruded and without life;
The eerie quiet pervades still, though, the patriots

Have abandoned the godhead, forsaken the bush paths
That led to palm wine camps, incensed bulrushes,
In search of distant cymbals and merriment

Set sail on the back of primed crocodiles
Ever yawning in sacred waters of the maker
Swollen squads of ruination on the sky-tide

II
One glowing morning, not long ago,
A village witch, dragged by a bemused father,
Swore at the shrine of *Tarakiri* at Ebedebiri[5]

Not to tamper with the wind blowing at the sails
This owl turned leaf, became a seer of elitist proportions
An iconoclast of the unseen realm, unmasking iron fraternities;

Her art thrived on a raw canvas, like O̲wo̲mu̲ O̲wo̲mu̲[6]
Calligraphing inverted phrases in the belly of twilight
Synthetic ditties hidden in strange moods and meandering

---

[5] A clan god.
[6] A Warri-based pastor and prophet

Then, a calabash spewed black air into living wombs
The mystical mirror at Ezebiri[7] showed a triumphant fate,
Defying all forms of grounding, or malevolent gravitas

Stained with a black speck in the soul;
Courting the mamba's lethal angst;[8] whoever raised
The rack so high mortals live on perpetual tiptoes

To futile ends, or remain buried
In a rosy mirage, a world without shape
Or sap; on the pulse of endless dreams,

Like an orphan in a house of many wives
Secretly nursing a sturdy white fate, undecipherable
From the chaos and hawks and restless bayonets?

Who says seers are beauties on the beach
Sluts on muddy winds – a fungoid fraternity excoriating
The bardic caste- a festival of ghommids and the heroic
    tortoise?

---

[7] A riverine community.
[8] The clan god's totem

THE LAMENT OF WATER HYACINTHS

A desert naked in the sun, feeds running meadows
Arousing inner ecstasy, in funerary song

Wakeful ardour of the soul, in risping recession
Whoever demurs bestrides a living stream

Notched in the blood, faggots which burn
In midnight, tinkering wearied joints in some turgid turf

In the hyacinths clasping her sibylline waters
Crawling in low tide; this is the place

Where encroaching sunlight touches the ground
Or is summoned to distil its vast silhouettes

Even beneath the tide where the fog
Is the pathfinder among rocks and stones;

Its seat is in the front row in the gallery
Of myth; an incantation grows in the mouth

To conjure the ghost of lost years
Whispering in extant ears of the wind

Broken in the beginning; to see through
The rainbow errors of song, one needs binoculars

Glazed rust needs some synthesis, to redeem
Its name among worthy kindred in an oasis

Fanning a clog of twisted fates
From the far ends of the wind

Strolling in silence, devouring resilient seaweeds
With no open whiff of resentment

With tingling suppleness, effluent conciliation
With no moral undercurrents; those juicy sauces

Are wasted in the bitterness of bile; the lament
Of water hyacinths pushed to dry land by tidal waves

A wry grin writhing in sun-scorched brownness
Arboreal dividends, in the smouldering silence

Which is no telltale of the famine floating
In the wind, confusing, like adulterated holy water

The ladder to heaven broken in the middle
A gnawing interregnum; who says nausea is a subaltern arse

Greed, a scavenger of empty calabashes
A plastered memory whose escapist edge

Is the smell of rusty iron in the wind?
Phosphorescent dreams fluster their wings

In motionless flight reaching an unripe orgasm –
The spilling of milk is a coming-of-age song

In the yellow glints of the sun; cocks now crow
Underground, a testament to the trumped-up wind

In claustrophobic spheres, even beneath the tide
There is a surfeit of kings with crowns

Or, at least, a king with a surfeit of iron-cast crowns
Prowling the length and breath of the green barn

Carrying overwhelming propositions clad in shadows
In precincts of maids wreathed with courtesy

In drinking joints; bottles that are never exhausted
Even with an elephant's multiple hearty lap

Into an empty belly, prompting a soulful probe
Into the wind, to divulge its memory

Jagged edges, potholes on narrow bends
The starving rites of seas

In robust silhouettes, lachrymal anecdotes
Lounging in fragrant hills, hollow pestrels

Luscious shrines that spray faceless prophecies in the air
Worshippers down on sore knees, like a grim penitent

Kissing the stations of the cross, not in snatches,
The full course at once, even without blinking

Which is a harpy indulgence of cowardice, mulling
Fanciful importunity; patriots though glazen

In outer parts, are full of soot, like ghosts
Meandering through market stalls in the dark

Scuttling the advantage of merchants
Malingering, somewhat obtuse, in a single direction

Their targets, standing in seductive tenderness
On red lanes, skimpy pants, sprawling...

AFTER THE WAR IN THE SOUL

The soul is stripped of her bold emptiness
After the war; the sneaky extravagance trimmed

Sunlight is screened on rocky ground
Crested wreakage in the air, arduous voice of thunder

Fading into water and ash in the whirling wind;
Men do not bemoan a squandered fate in a hurrying tide

The muezzin's lament does not ruffle blue blood
It swells in the dour circle of dwarfs and sycophants

The funeral cloth summons the shadowy sage
The sleep-laden eyes see like hippos in the night

Pulsing in their dimness, surge of the way,
To the eye-catching epitaph, shorn of living waters

Unspoken melodies are barred from the wind
Only patriots overhear something like a synthetic crow

The imprimatur of shrivelling cocks, a worthless adjunct
Wrenched from the stars; ablution does not brook
grandstanding

You do not ring a bell to summon a market; this earth
Scents of acrid, if you keep your nose to the ground;

So much territorial instincts, like *Ogidisibe-owei*[*],
Guardian of the Amassoma backyard

---

[*] A small deity at Amassoma.

The uncannily huge frame of a spirit man
In a white wrapper, carrying a machete

Instilled eerie scare in the winding bush path to Ogobiri[+]
Encompassed by deep green vegetation and the wild

A white scarf tied around the peak
Of a standing pole a symbolic representation;

So much walking with the head
Peeing in sacred groves; so much tortoise shit

In the brain; black rain wraps a white cloth
On the face of the wind, seeking conciliation

The crescent light is voided by the unseen lust
Roaming the streets; awake to the fire

Nestling in the home; patched promises
Howling in the sea; fresh debts of banquet halls

Bankrupt cathedrals divine the past
Busy probing the Godhead, the flowery myth

Ghosts decree the direction of the tide
Stars swarm the sidewalks, down the debris

Mingling with marsh, the fast-laden wind
They wear posh cassocks, teasing the flock

Paint the moonlight in the blood with grey strokes
A steady monody when the day goes to sleep

[+] Adjoining town to Amassoma.

The white spirit has abandoned the earth
At the riverside, ungatherable feathers adorn the noontide

A synthetic harvest; rotted in the roots
Maggots pulsate the breasts, clutching the fleeing green

And sunlight abandons the altar
Distilled in unwritten complexities

No one gathers grains on inveterate rocks and stones
Or chattering company in the shadows

Sceptres sold in the ballot to brown blood
Fulfil the scripture of misted foliage riding the skies

The mystical sap notched in waves
Weaves the crowns of the earth

Sinking on the day of coronation
Or flung far to blistering bulrushes

In the village grove; the green sold
To solitary foothills, leaning on telltale cowries

Vain cognomens rend the air, chirrupy,
Cloying in stashed wealth in vaults far away

Which thresh the fate of sunken rainbows,
Slashed sins posted on overcast stars

The calcified arteries of remnants of salted souls
After the war; lustrous spirits sold in the market-place

In spirit, by somnolent sages sitting
On stumps, in the void, with errant arses.

GOING DOWN WITH THE SUN

When vultures and owls encircle a haven at the riverside
Gleaming in the peeking sun, the blood has k-leg
At best, a cortege of covert dreams

When sages sit on termite-infested stumps
In lantern shades in the ancient hearth
The offspring crumble under the weight of debt

In the household; squabbles rend the air
Over a vainglorious inheritance, sins stacked
In the midday heat, lifeless, like cockroach carcasses

Swept away by the whirlwind in the dark
Where souls drift away in the open sea
Falling to the fireflies which light up the heart

The high tide great on reverse fins, the tassels of loft
Razed down in the unwholesome glint
Stuck on glittering dregs of blood

Towering waves go down with the sun
Spiralling in the wind, the dusty antennae of dusk
In the wanton acrobatics of monkeys

In throbbing tropical forests, leaning
On the sixth instinct; rather imperceptively
The moonbeams illuminate the splashing shoregrass

Inviting grandma to the river till twilight
Stifling the famished fate of contrived outcasts
Hearts sunken when the river falters in its laden flow

Beyond the clouds hanging in the horizon
Cloying in an intangible web, the suckling
Iron-traps of praise-singing carnivores

A shadow is lost in solitary bush paths
In daylight, not gurgling neighbourhoods
Beyond the preachments of earthly priests

The faeces of chameleons haunt the air
The moonbeams smile on the wilderness
Threshing a miracle in the wild

We do not need a diviner to know
The colour of ripe mango
Beyond the open roots shrouded

From the bedraggled sunbird, otherwise
Cacophonous on the summit of palm tress
Watered by twilight dews, hanging in season

On the horizon, a sultry leper-house
With multiple nuggets of catechumen,
Grey hurricanes, straying from the powerhouse

The pyramid of opaqueness, sanitizers
Of abstruse playgrounds of long dehydrated stars
Beyond sensuous love games at midnight

Trapping healthy fragments of God's breath
Upholder of the cosmos of being, congealed
By the steamy cold troubling the sun

Bringing the empire down to the pit
Where maggots hold sway in rampant sketches
On the navel, for numbing clues in the air.

THE END-POINT

The end-point is a starveling moonshine
A flawed farewell in the middle of nowhere
A fateful festival in the reckoning of mermaids

Palm fronds take over the streets, the shadows
Walking with heads, like oil workers
The bonfire in dour slovenly blood reaches its peak

Stripped of green leaves and myth
An enchanting turpitude, which springs
From dark soil, a castaway in its glory

A living cycle, elemental fabrications
Heaped on oily heads, compost of muddied moist
A monstrous miasma in a magnificent moment

Acting out a sly script under tropical moons
The breath full of questions;
The depositions full of sticky worms

Though in gilded apparel, armed with luscious rhetoric
Owner of the godhead; a crackling vocation
In an ineffable moment, etched in memory

Roaring empires dissolve into ash
In their peak; a village belle
Wrinkles and bow-bends in eventide

A life-long festival is squandered
On the trappings of wayward breasts
Tottering towards self-immolation in whorls of whirlwind

A surging pulse buried in the incandescence
Of night, the shrillness of bulbuls
The halcyon infiniteness of virgins

Forced into a union; a suffocating closet
In the sea, slashing the promise flowering
In the horizon, like a full moon

The brusqueness and spasm and pure prism
Spread out in the sun, like cassava flakes
By Urhobo women; so supple with seasoned fish

An unrepentant thief suffers a gory fate in fluvial spheres
A heavy stuff is hung on his neck
And thrown into the wild sea,

The ripples dark and endless; a sticky memorial
Of green leaves darkening the sky
The heavens shrink, wrinkling the young

Who are scared stiff; their voices slithered
In the towering waves assailing the shores
Acrid receptacles; gratuitous devils, hoary estrangement

A tremulous cold in the homely essences
Of a mermaid's embrace; who does not know
Tidal waves remind us of earth's wet beginnings?

The savoury never-ending banquets
The route to nirvana through labyrinthine thighs
Chauffeur of dizzy heights, ponderous stones

Fleecing motions and medals in parliament
Clotting the sea breeze in the sun
A callused moonwalk, like a slovenly courtier

A fake pregnancy, to hook a man
On high seas whose head never touches
The ground; tangible and ominous

Like the unsettling clustering of con merchants
In a secret grove; odorous,
Like the brine of a he-goat.

THERE IS NO RED TALE IN HEAVEN

There is a tale of red flowers and pitfalls
Engraved, without seams, in the southerly winds;
Human blood is white before birth
Hemmed in by broken petals, destitute fortresses

Numb courtyards, without juice or lustre
Where the food served by fate is bland and brackish
And comes at odd hours, oft
With a nauseating essence, when hunger

Gnaws at the blood to her fill, overturning
The messianic miasma of abiding moonshines
In the stomach, or in the aroused world
In darkly clasps, in warm company.

Providence is oft presented in a fatuous light
Inherently flawed or partial in her monarchical judgement
Which appears in flinty droves, sweaty and soothing
At once, in the brimming lust in tambourines

The dishevelled blood drives dreams of the waist
Surging to the head in potent, extravagant spirals
Like mountainous waves buzzing on sweltering shores
The spoils of breath unleashed on the drowning fire

The moistened parch, the arcane fart
In the open air; anonymous or whose name
Fouls the mouth; broad and luscious in the wind
Like cocoyam leaves sprouting on a garbage dump

Blazing through the filth, the acrid odour
Soiling the length and breadth of the globe
Prompting a motionless stampede, green confessions,
Jocund intimations in a sacred grove

Ascending invisible stairways to the edge
Of paradise; the soul is inflated in the fullness
Of furrows and facades in the market place
The underbelly of the sea enfolds its seedy secrets

Shimmering shadows, fragrant graveyards
Visceral silences, menacing and slothful high-rise waves
Sensuous heartbeats spreading dew on wrinkles
A chaotic tango of opposite blood at the beams

Like mangoes forced to ripen, entering
A treasure-house through the back door
A sanctimonious flirtation with bonfires of the soul
Subterranean strides; strifing gestures at Christmas

A damsel succumbs to amorous overtures in water
Her feet draw some undecipherable hieroglyphics
Suckling a loaded mind; breeds a leprous hug
Which clears obdurate weeds in the wind

A portentous renewal of a primitive disharmony
A delectable predator disses kernels of love –
The mark of virtuoso blood; impervious
To towering waves assailing the canoe

In the middle of River Forcados;
A clustering of tumid satiation
In all the senses; fecund furrows are always
Wrung out of love in a wrong place.

THIS GREEN IS HOLLOW

Shadows of waters squander the halo of God
In high places; the horizon saunters into waves
And hollow greens, into charred flesh
Hidden in the smog-abiding abysm of daylight.

There is no aperture for roving sunlight
To sneak in those vestiges of potent ash at noon
Pulsating undiminished in the open closet
Horrid surplices, the death dance of flinty worlds

Where footmarks of marauders set the pace, nameless,
Serenade the sleepy streets at sundown
Drowning inane footfalls of priests
In their offals, a fardel of fiery fire

Filtering souls long gone sour, full of swag
In a burst of aphrodisiacal umbrage
Starveling stillness and sweat
In the midst of dizzy beauties

Cadavers roam the moon, not the spirit world
Which is, itself, an open estrangement;
A bastion of breezy knots, based on the stomach,
Blind their visions and roadmaps

Groundless in their grounds, which they make public
In a splintering spree of soulful songs;
The hard, irreducible sanctuary packaged for extended blood
Is effaced by cool, flowing waters...

This is the science of self-denial
Where the self and others dance different dances
In sunlight; the tongue cannot
Ambush the teeth in a war of blood

Siring a dreamy field of wreaths
Whitening the earth; the expansive sea
Caressed by southerly winds powers the bard
Of unsightly foliage, dressed in Sunday clothes

Stalking forerunners on the pages of the sun
In remotest hinges, beyond the searing spear;
A muted animosity is a hollow hymn
Sung late in the choir in holy matrimony.

The fire gathers sparks, grows taproot
The flowers and fruits sparkle
Unassailably in the wind, seducing
The heathen with unleavened bread

Or an open pool of brine; intoxicating
Apostasies spew from blazing hues,
The pubescence of covenly pews;
A passionate lover wastes her wares in a brothel

Sniffing around for imaginary cracks, seeking
Fleecy orgasm in a graveyard; clients bewitch her nipples
With inordinate praises and the raddle of rank romance
Reaching uncharted corners of the world.

A PLASTERED MEMORY

Love is a sweltering curse
Full of fireflies; a plastered memory
Gurgling at the seams; a griot in prison
With many escapist edges.

The power of the sun is defiant
Over dinghy stones and watermarks
Smell of rusty iron in the wind;
Chirrupy sea birds in endless song

Primal strifes sink the earth
Phosphorescent dreams fluster their wings
In faked orgasm - the spilling of milk
Is a coming-of-age song, heard in the blood

Cocks crow underground in overcast skies
Trumped-up winds in claustrophobic spheres
Ablution brooks no grandstanding or rigmaroles;
You do not ring a bell to summon a market

This earth smells of arm-pit acrid
If you keep your nose to the ground;
So much walking with ant-infested heads
Peeing on sacred groves, without being pressed

So much tortoise shit in the brain, turning human blood,
Ravaging green reserves; and white rain
Wraps a funeral cloth on the face of the earth
The light of the sun voided by the unseen lust

Roaming the streets; a slew of warriors
Carry palm fronds on the highway
Posting facades on fate that live in the senses;
Phoney colours, visceral odours...

This cyclone of dust blurs ethereal voyeurs;
Whosoever proclaims purity in a tortoise's mute fart
Taunts the open hands of providence-
There is no miracle in a misstep debasing the carrion

Ravishing the head even before the starting point;
Somewhere in the dark, in the heartland,
Childhood dreams are damned daily
On charred haunches in the morning dew

With thunderous glee and clapping of hands
Succulent damsels on hand to grease their lions;
The hedgerow favours valediction, spreading love
On hot sand dunes and tasteless meadows.

UPTURNING THE EARTH'S METAPHYSICS

Cocoyam sprouts on black-faced manure
In desolate dumps at Ogwashi-uku;
Onion on odorous cow-dung:
The metaphysics of this earth in full blaze

Maniacal droplets of dew massage her womb
When the world snores away in lovers' clasps;
No cock chokes in the loudness of its crow
The burden of waking up a wearied clan

A slovenly storehouse of indeterminate dreams
Heights laden with petrel and birdsong,
Fade into oblivion right by the fire of grandma's hearth
The fissures of a daylight voyeur

Picking the bones of absence
Where boulders and beams prop up
The shadow of being fossilized in the blood,
Sometimes unmalleable; always in a hurry

Destined to cross the shoreline in leapy latchets
Overtaking the ponderous antelope in the forest
With a breezy prophecy, suffused in her entrails;
Fellow ticklers of war canoes, defamed in the outposts

Harbouring scurrilous stuff, in crisp wraps
Mournful bells ring in the horizon without end
In dizzying harmony; in the end, a cosy marmalade
Carries anonymous caskets from an imaginary hearse

Through the village square, exposing
Man's lashed fate in gathering clouds
Over sweet-smelling shrubs, full of synthetic fruits,
Furrowed leafage, like a leprous hug in broad daylight;

Boundless, like an invading kiss of waters
On acquiescent river banks, mellowing
Down heartbeats ashore, trickling
Peddles and padlocks in counterpoise

In ancient regimentals, showing up in assorted species
Suckling the sloth hollowed out in the middle;
Even a full dose of milk on wetted garri
Cannot drown their drunken essence

Eons of miles away from the earth
At the moment of reckoning, the lugubrious cannons
Grease importunate blood, always exuding arrogance
Like one wearing twenty *Olorogun*[*] headpieces.

---

[*] Ayakoromo masquerade

SURROGATES OF THE SOUL

Earthy surrogates glaze over the odorous smell
Of rotten shrubs and the tilapia head
Floating in posh precincts.

The liberal wind, plangent women
Draughty in their dreams, the eagle
Fluttering her wings midair, bugs knotted

To glorious stuff, poignant in their secret pleas
The white pigeons and palm fronds they flaunt
Under moonbeams, fuel the myriad famished groins

On moist earth, overgrown with cactus
Their souls fused in the crucible of prickled dreams
Hiding a horde of snakes in deep green herbage

The dreams of lads posted in trenches
Glancing through the famished wind
Scented dreams spurt from muddied earth

Cairns of prized sweat from the womb, age-long
Shadows perch on the scalding blossom of the wind
The crude splashes of River Forcados sag the soul

And the evening heralds the ascension of cockerels
To plantain leaves which, suckled by metallic sleep,
Announce another break of day in the calcified clime

A dying craftsman, clinging to the wind -
No tears sprout over exposed sugar besieged
By the tyranny of ants, straining over

The burgeoning passions of priests, decanters
Of floundering impulses, painters of a demurring canvas
Abrasive to hidden breasts and grains

In darkling barns, or buffets of bums
The rock can spurt a torrent of living waters
In intimate tenderness; an escape route

From the white touch of ordained priests
Odorous tinsels who limit the speed of light
Assegais of webs, foil of doodling dew

Stark and convoluted, in a sparkling way
Contending with the rays of blood, at the foot
Of green mountains, swallowed by the abiding smog

In the horizon, which swallows the rustling
Twilight breeze; furrowed beings hustle in vain
In raped fragrances, the beehive caught up in unseen clouds

Fishermen saunter riverward with bowls
Of net on padded heads in vain when night starts
To remove her dark duvet from the face of the earth.

THE CARCASS OF A RIVER

Deep dimples are not on pilgrimage
On grandma's face; they mark the glowing years
Of twilight, weary grace, masculine mellowness
When dew-cold hung in the morning mist
Thawed on cloud-drenched earth; ashes of souls

Crushed in the creviced green of chameleons
Glorious ducklings in a cosy morning swim
At Amatebe waterside;[*] but who can simulate indifference
To the glassy rot buried in the humongous womb
Of silence, wrenches of mad bazaars sprinting
Down the spine, the highway to God

That boasts of sterile ends? Always,
My mind wanders to virgin forests at Ogwashi-uku
Freshly mowed down for a road
To the new world when, as kids
At the end of the seventies, we hung

On slack climbers on still-standing trees (and boulders)
Swaying rhythmically in the obsequious air
The dizzy throbbing blood dredged the fun
The fragrance of blossoming fruits, the earthy warmth
Of green all around us, callow souls
The midday sun exuded a sinewy luminousness

The enchanting blood turning golden hues
Engrafted in the thin scattered shades in the grove
The coaxing songs of winged beings, the choir of green.
Now there is a masked glimmer in the horizon
Soulful vultures with rolling eyes protect

---

[*] A quarter in Bomadi

Living carcasses, a dang of dinghy darkness
In thickets cackling with clipped wings
A plague of constellations rout the sweetness of blood,
Implacable, like *Olorogun*[*] on the prowl; intoxicated
By the flawless rendering of plumed verse
Gauging the palm of Sunday congregations.

The mellow pulse of star-lit nights
Exposing sagging breasts, shadows suitably on point
The hearty exultation of a tyrant's dungeon
The painted full tide carrying waterlilies
On her broad shoulders, the carcass of a river.

---

[*] Ayakoromo masquerade

ESTRANGEMENT

A turbulent temper, yet-unexplored night airs
Brooking no alibis, or the absence of straws
Or undiluted honey, in the wind;
A willing receptacle of hermetics held up
By the abundance of abstract love

The lunar canvas is the rump that scatters
The spine of sages, hidden suns in open seas
A foreknowledge of the abject corrosiveness
Of sulphur is a fragrant memory-
An overarching incandescence scribbled

In sultry syllables, etching the sagacity of burnished souls
A wreathed contrivance in high places
A whishing tower; mellifluous ramshackles
In government reserved quarters; healthful flowers
Dance to their death in the hot wind

Temples tick with heavy incense and necropolis
In the city centre, long honed in satiny points
The glowing elegance of black blondes who prefer
A colour transmigration into some faded hue –
Uncouth and languid and acidulous

A misguided monging for quotidian rainbows
Full of cain-yam holes; incorrigible pustules
Of virginal passes, a ruminant canvas
Of human harpoon that needs some whittling down

A strange, putrified pearl in the breastbone
Swollen claws threshed in the moon
A silvery swagger, brimming with calcareous grit

A bludgeoning, finical carrion encircles the mind
In visceral lustres, marooned in a strange sea
Furrows whirling the leprous waters in the middle
In an aromatic, uncompromising drift to the wild

The indenture is continually replenished
The desecrated gauntlet full of cheer
The indeterminate heritage of predators

Naked rickshaws, lacklustre circumlocutions
Of an unyielding toaster having emptied
The commonwealth; trodden torpors of black tyrants
Who cow or stem living waters

With their uncouth orbits, extant squalls
A heart of guilt is as heavy as lead
Flounders in unslippery hemispheres.

The comely crosscurrents of camphor
Fragrant poplars teetering in stony crevices
Tawny bits of primitive egos bystanders may not see,
Gnawing away the foliage of the soul in moonlight.

A GHOST'S FOOTMARKS

This shadow hanging on the horizon
Without end, sprouts from tawdry winds
Taking the labyrinthine route to a dove's tomb
A ghosts tangled crush, without footmarks

To behold the grove's god under the unction
Of some preening priest, so subtle and harpy
And frontal and fiercely territorial
Like the don hippo, all at once.

Let's go to the village market
Wherein echoes empty dreams wrapped
In deep green leaves; the bulbul's
Well-rehearsed shriek; the redeemers' choir

Who upturn the table on a cobra's darkly head
But open the gate for delinquents to flood the pulpit
Invisible worms ravishing ears of maize –
The inverted earth is the tyrant's trench

Needs no trigger to foil avowed havens
The unpretentious patchwork in the wind
The white sheets swaddling their pulse;
Every pain has a cure in the bush

Even stasis, or the latescence of a snail's strides
Until windy breath leaves its ancestral home willy-nilly
And glorious annotations adorn the tomb
The streets witness shrill drums and voice

Witness ostentations unguents packaged
Across days and nights, to the soothing
Plough of wind's pores through naked waves
The orifice of blood absolves itself of probe

Paints the horizon with chaotic ornaments
Eternal tuberous argosies bequeathed to the sons
Of the chosen; not shifting, ownerless vestments
Sold in the black market, in noonshine

We must stay awake to take stock of the song
On the misted hill top abiding in the soul
The mildewed ministry outside the gospel of life
Which boasts of tabernacles laden with incense.

ADDENDUM

There is no addendum to the sacred word
The unseen symphony in the wild
Unfailing fragrance of moonflowers
No undiscovered truths in purgatory

No sanction in the swollen strides of penitents
Though they ooze the sequined blood of the earth;
Songs of brotherhood carry hidden fire
The smell of burnt essences in their crescendo

Feed the comely horizons of butchers
Of the common patrimony; patriots and priests
Buried seedlings lurch through the misty earth
Into suave flowers at dawn, ladder to eternal life

The putrid, unkempt mad man of Amatebe[*]
In the late seventies, trudging without aim
Gloating at sizzling moments swaying in the wind
Ripe as mango fruits, unseen by full-blooded mortals

A glorious memory conjures a benighted granary
Outer piety cannot host the gifts of God
Eternal pedants, though crushing upon the crescent moon
Like passing a death sentence on the dregs

Of the earth, or a charge of foul blood
Averse sounds from the pangs of peppered genitals
A curfew on harlequins, pandering
To the dark darts of a lad accused

---

[*] A quarter in Bomadi

Of wetting an orthopaedic foam overnight
Where night men announce their agenda in noon lightning
Striking cables of blood in their primal fluorescence
In barren gates, coursing to a rotund glow

In the sacred depths of Agbaya bou,[*] home of
Hibernating birds haunted out of dappled nests
The timeless secrets of light years
Untrammelled flight in the obsequious air.

Envy floats in plangent undercurrents
Potent in its muted intensity, like iron-wood
Heaving in its underground cell a flotilla
Of unseen arrows in the muddy air

Encircling the living orchard, the ripe
Pomegranate quivering in her stalk
A cold wind blows past, seeking
A soulful conjugation, wearing a serpent's face.

---

[*] A mystical forest.

THE MIRACLE OF BREATH

I

A long day postpones its end without end
The lengthy shadow of love spreads its rainbow propositions;
Hush green shrubs, full of redeeming propensities
Foul the lambent air, awry seeds sprout in cathedral gardens

A garish beauty, as abhorrent as a bug-infested bed
A sizzling smoked goldfish full of maggots

The miracle of breath heavy on the chest of believers
This grove of ghosts, nattering cage, open knots,
The interspaces promptly shut to sunlight
Oblivious a barred door is nothing to a ghost

The river must grow steel in her voice
In rapturous current, in moments of placid strides

Or when the waters gloriously brim up the banks
Their dinghy orifice, reticence stills the air
Shadowy souls pee on flowers, like a goat
Gloss over human blood spurted from seasoned souls

Blooms are always hobbled in imperial mists
Like a snake in perplexed stillness,

Listening hard for telltale signs in the air
The greenness of a sacred grove, sometimes,
Lures us to lust; the estranged lover,
Struggling with hard things, mocks

Twilight in lonely street corners, dusky
In their vaulting apparel, arcane fragrances.

II

The smell of rotted fart is a tingling memory
In the obtrusively dank wind
A naughty anus' baggage
That courts public opprobrium.

Leafless boughs ensnare the moon
The votary spine of sagging flesh
Distraught tenants resort to ecumenical claws
Unheeding the plumy cascades of dawn

In virgin forests, shaved or smouldered
By distinguished throngs, with colourful topics
In the air, mired in glinting dust
Shrouded in white, loomed in dainty thread

How does one push an unwilling churchman
To sacramental catechism, moaning over fleeced
Banquets and ghosts, invoke thunderbolts of verbiage,
Poised as a leopard's snarls, in pregnant protest?

A savage sepulchre crystallizes in complicit folds
The nibbling yearning of a muezzin
A dim crested crouch, compelling circumspection
In the wild, hovering over forlorn riversides

The cobra is notched to the wind, mottling growth
Which dissolves in water, like bile,
Hovering over rhymes of blood
Like a fangled vulture in frenzied flight

Frozen in the womb of a faithless dream:
A sacred bath cannot stop bouts of malaria fever
A pitiable paunch asphyxiating tantrums
A borderless spool of blizzards in the marketplace

In the face of a raucous silence, in patronizing gestures,
In synthetic counterpoint, the wanton perspiration
In the midst of healthful air conditioners
The smoky iridescence of subterranean games.

SAGGING STARS

There is a cycle of sagging stars, limbering crocodiles
Burdened by the wind's capricious streaks
The showy shrouds, cocoyam leaves on steel,
Lost in some nitwit nipple, somewhere in midday

A wet pilgrim thaws on dark flesh,
Like the nebulous contours of a god's face;
O memory is an eternal furrow without
Reversal or cure, no gnawing interregnum

No moonlit hide-and-seek, no phantom fireflies!
Who would not be seduced by the harpy halo,
The tickling inscapes, all streaks of shadows,
Fat promises, woven with wind and ash?

Now to the days of immanent fluorescence
Hidden in God's own temple, cruising ahead
Of the canoe of fate; the buried sap
Brims with green fire and lightning

An unheard siren in somnolent waters
In the camp of silhouetted saints, bearers
Of blooming pendants; who can tell
The story of green cornfields in flooded farmlands?

A drenched fowl careers in open closures
The hanging heist - as scary as seven owls
Flying away from one spot, exchanging
Low, knowing shrieks, serving notice of crossroads

Havens sink garish souls in tepid waters
The streets as smelly as a rotted tilapia head
Host blood-shot eye-lashes; lichened underpants
Grow bold in secret, trudging on bare feet

Repelled by the white promise of the beginning
Lost in sour grapes and catwalk

Withered dreams suddenly gather light
Limping to the shadow, with the certitude
Of a timeous orgasm, without a tinge of sapor,
Enamoured of cactus or scorching heat

The weird secrets of water creatures are buried
In the crocodile's stomach, not a premeditated vertigo
    threshing

Lost on the road to the sky in the unblinking
Glare of sunlight, alien to drought - no toddler can
Scan the loins of River Forcados; There is a festival
Unseen, rasping in the void, carrying the charm of anonymity

It is not for nothing hippos and lions rest by day, hunting
At night; their visions burnished by night's dark veil

The ageless watchman of the passage
To the depths of unswerving foothills
Swoops on celebrated husks; bits of wind
And harlequins play on the waters of light.

MOCKING THE GODHEAD

Those who go straight to the point
In blood games, slouching in a whirlpool,
Without preambles, invite exhaustion,
Or lays wreaths on the waist before dawn.

Preambles prepare the grove before a plunge
Mellows the veins for a throaty birdsong
Throbbing in the depths of the soul
The meeting-point of earthly suns.

The burden of the wagtail stills the senses
In the undergrowth silent, in solicitude; the swollen ego
Of beach sand numb to strains in the wind
Unbruised by mounting waves in moonlight.

The distraction of approaching footsteps, crampy
Voices, fretful shrouds over watchtowers of dreams
The scattered fate of the prodigal
Suppliant thunder, in gruelling spree, in the open air

Anarchy breathes with joy in the revelations
Beyond the eye-catching plume of the peacock;
The soul of man rules the stones, the incurable
Extravagance of shadows, niggling nightmares

The phantom floodgates, bulbuls in endless shriek
The birthright of pilfering on the altar of God
Thighs wide open in the middle of prayers
Deep-throated, even without a whimper

Nowadays God's unction dwells in open derelicts
The gangling reverie, tongues stoking
(Un) usual places in daylight, mocking the Godhead
The noiseless strides of faecal maggots –

The stairway to dancing nude in the spirit
And there is a fulsome hope shadows would resurrect
Before the fullness of the season, in time
To avoid damnation, in rotten corners of the shrub!

A stained purity, in tumid enchantment
With the errors of dinosaurs, nothing changes
Nothing irredeemable, the twisted glory in the wind
The same old smell of unwholesomeness.

If the root is dyed in drift, the soul
Ascends to the bottom of a muddied pool
Without grace or gall, stretching far in a closet
Humped in unending want in moonglow.

The still hanging air needs sanctification,
To wrench cascades of faeces
From the soul of earthy saints –
The broom must sweep

Beyond the corridors, fostered
With a commodious motto –
Not the fanciful fouling
Of estranged camps

Not the menacing pee on tawdry cracks
Of the cathedral wall, the gaping potholes
On the road to heaven, nor the wanton bombs
That scatter on tender sunflowers in the sun

Swaddled with sacramental stone, misplaced,
Like a barren home team serenaded
Unto the pitch, only to be denied windfalls
Stacked in wrong corners of the earth.

BLACK PULCHRITUDE

The owners of raucous laughter, tumescent airs,
like a crab; wild in the spirit, numb to blood,
Enter town, to a triumphant cheer.

Sublimals of a busy year of wandering exploits
Roll to a halt; buried in their hearts
Is a whore who wove a path for saints
To tread to heavensgate at twilight.

Dinosaurs scheme in their tombs
Buried with one leg flailing outside
Wearied by crossfires of rain and sun

The discontent abiding in the mottled air
In patriots' dry pockets in the rainy season –
This earth rests on the shadows of a dream
Tattooed in the wind or a fast-flowing tide

Riddled with the smell of rotted fart
Blowing from unnameable ends
Crashing in full season, into musty fragments

Bag carriers for patriots bulge at the seams
Wholly visible in their secret crumbs
Swollen in the awning brotherhood and bond
The abscesses of ghosts ooze in the wind

Termites feed fat on burrowing
The earth in search of living corpses
Wakes to a festival of white tongues

Sensual inhibitions in noontide
Forged in air-conditioned tabernacles
The converse sides of coins converge
To purchase God in honey markets

So long the queue of willing merchants
The dove does not wait for clement winds
On tree tops for eternity, to show off

Those majestic strides on nature's brown carpets.
The bulbul prophesies to a deaf throng
Hanging multiple passports to paradise
On bloated necks – blooming flowers in full season

In a dark room of fanciful skeletons
Which startle the gatekeepers of ancient cults
Always in festal habiliments, long robes,

The eyes stark-red, the mouths oozing
The hangover of dusk-to-dawn booze
Heavy with pendants on their necks
Fiercely territorial, like the don hippo

Counting American dollars like palm kernel
Just a little revelation at the forge:
The spirit of man and flower are entwined

The tomb a mere token enclosing the chaff
The killing of a butterfly playing on nectar leaves
Spells eternal dimples on the spirit of mortals
The world thrives in thickets of dark fantasy;

Put forth a wrong foot in a dream, to stem
The sea of sharks; become a legend of doggerel
And thunder, not flowing streams feeding

Drooping flowers on the shore, lost to the seduction
Of mermaids; the bat's vision stitches up the season
Lying in garish fragments and bandages –
Keyword for the burning cathedral at noon.

COSMOPOLITAN WISDOM

Basking in the lavender whims of the world
I build legends with broomsticks in the wind
Razing down ancestral groves untouched all ages
Living secrets of the sacred palm fronds

In *Odele*'s shrinehouse, unfurled at sunset
To do the pantheon's bidding,
On the pleas of pilgrims
On the prompting of a receding day

Fade into a dump site, in a dour pose
For the archival camera, and vultures
Square on a toddler's stuttering journey
Bearing toys that have long ceased to play

The souls of festivals dissolve into tombstones
Like early morning dew on leaves
When noon beams her yellow light
On the route to salted hips on the back

Of obsequious plantain shrubs, darkly scented
Like the fluid of living groves
In the awning drizzle, fanning
The gathering moon in the blood

Running like high tide in River Forcados
A corpse strolls with exuberance
At the village waterfront, a mangled flow,
Basks in the bounties of the sun

A tormented lad sits in the front row
Of the cathedral, with a wry smile
Scarcely covering the bundle of doubtful hope
A caged canary serenades the acquiescent crowd –

Passport to the intrepid harmonies of brotherhood
What pilgrim comes before *Odele*[*]
To tease out the fire in the ancient hearth
To stalk polarized wiles of the enemy

In his own celestial camp, fanning
Nocturnal targets with a big long hat,
Without holding a dog, slaughtered
With a stroke of the machete,

Like lightning, by an *Ogbu*[+] cult member
Set apart in the feathers stuck to the head –
Sign of the number of bloody sins in the season –
And the looming red apparel in an all-white *Ogele*[π]

Three times across the village foresquare;
Presages of eternal unrest, on gurgling foothills
The burdened harvest of silence,
Ferment of faceless flutes

An impalement: the tortoise's guided exuberance
Woven into alluring dark clay bowls
The willowy rasps hollering in the wind
Tame the dream of rivers, otherwise

Fussy on a mermaid's bedchambers
The engulfing dance and promise
In a graveyard, pierce the acrid void,
Like the medic's prompt pin

---

[*] A god at Ayakoromo, Delta State, Nigeria.
[+] A village cult.
[π] Procession.

For a blood sugar test before sunrise
Ecstatic in dawn's distended gongs
Cuddling the prophecy in the wind,
Like a willing mistress under harmattan duvets

Faith now grovels and fluffs, manacled
To mute wavecrests that dwarf
The hippo's thunderous bellow; stitches
The mild whims of the world to a surging brushfire.

WHITE DEBRIS

Gleaning white flowers litter the graveside
At the village cathedral, without siren; horsemen
Of great tidings, wafted into the wind, straining

Against the surging threshold amplifying
The message of the town crier
Lubricants of the hearth, without libation

We shrug off impalements in green prickles
Of the earth, bred in anonymous markets
The revolving amnesty, hatchery of conspiracies

Whoever mocks the reign of meandering minstrels
Immaculate entrails whose light engrafts
A graveyard cold in the veins, awaiting

The ripe bush mango to fall in the depths
Of the throbbing earth where the curved waist
Of a woman drinks perduring communion?

Suddenly, the world is a whirlwind
Of babbling songs, resonant in the head
Revolving around distant winding mountains

Each moment a wakeful secret, distilled
By the impregnable light of the white sea
Her waves, the epicurean chauffeur

Guided by moonlight; the sky, painted
In highfalutin strokes, the ebbing bond
Between teeth and tongue

The broken thirst for our other selves
Cringing on green hillsides, far-flung
Or withering sand bays in sun-scorch

The boiling arguments down River Forcados
Shell short-changed; the hydro-carbon blackness
Raped fishermen's libations dare not heal;

Blood awakens to countless crossroads
The mounting mounds scattered across the Delta
Blood recedes into a numbskull in a delirium

Long shadows accompany the blue waves, like
A heavy dose of dope prickling naked fates of seafarers,
The perverse grimace, like the tongue of a roasted dog

There is no spliced seed to grow the streets
Of sand dunes, carrying the burden of shaved skyscrapers
The contorted acquaintance with rueful remnants

Of the massacre of blood; bats flapping wings
Against annealed walls, threatening
To withdraw the sun from the desert

When a house is fallen, goats defecate on rooftops
Famished stars inscribed on stones, like bowels
Carrying sour stuff, the living testimony

Tainted tongues crack the sanctity
Of the umbilical cord; the cacophony
Of crystals bearing a common name

In cultic spheres, repository of brilliant ornaments
Of the roving earth nocturnal in spirit
Though a certified freeborn of oilfields.

A RESONANT VOID

I
A winding mist blends into the void
Obstructing the free flow of the wind
Like anguished stones piled on the vocal tract

No offals or potions, an absolute virgin lust
From the masked choir; the master, pot-bellied

There is no screaming in underground skies
The weight of the elephant's thud shuts up all
A resonant stillness hangs in the surrounding palms

Wanders in the belly of the river, itself quivering
On the back of an impulse heavy and acrid

A steaming cold befriends the wind late in the day
A queer creature, summoned from the realm of myth,
Laments the tumultuous descent of blood

A discourteous breed making a mockery of ribald stones
A lonesome counsel limps in the wind

The crowd enchanted by the bankruptcy
The caterpillar takes to every leave in the bush
The garlanded fiat, the comely curse of the chosen species

The black road that unclads dreams of loft and song
A white cradle begets a raving twilight, the distillation

Of chirping crickets on dry beaches in the early morning sun;
Supple, plum, untrammelled, primed in the mere being
The river rippling in fulsome delight

The whirlpool of *Ofenibenghan** humming,
Glistening on the cover page of the deep

A niggling shade for the soul of man
The origin of impalpable breath, procreant
Of effusive sweetness and bile in the blood

A bulging perfection, dimmed by mindless plunges
Which underline a claim to the secrets of the earth

A mere redoubling of her powers; all farce
And fog, growing grey beard in the young day
Or calcified in the wind, host of ageless myths

II
The tender yolks of the beginning
Are always carking rubbles at dusk

Soiled in the putrid waters flowing
Through streets without drainages, as if
To catch up with something in the next street

Draped sunbeams etch a gurgling dross
Clamouring for epitaphs on living tombstones

Death whimpers on the sidelines, in dumb trumpets
Sometimes, incomprehensibly, in a sign language
Empty of prophecy, a bile in the barn

The sun's distance, too, is nothing, though with a price;
Fluid, uninhibitive dust hanging in the air

---

* Also known as "Okrika", a riverine Ijo community in Delta State of Nigeria.

A star bard harps on the exit route
From crossroads; bursts the barricades
On the road to love and the barn

Mounted by souls in white masks
The flare, tactile and searing, forbids illusion

And the nostrils, not flattered, absorbs cobwebs
All the dark affirmations littering little dreams
A bedlam of sweet strayings, in the depths

Of the open sea; shimmering scorpions provide
A footmat at twilight, blurring dissolute

Arguments about man's origins, limping towards
A doughty destination, of counterfeit tweak
In the blood, in the grip of common claws

A militant impulse spreads gingerly over virgin rubbles
Going up up in crackle and smoke and stench

And the coy wind labours in vain in the circumstance
To stem the surge, on the slew of prompted
Warmongers, carrying palm fronds on the high way.

A SETTLED BANKRUPTCY

A bankrupt soul dazzles in speculation, leaning
On green memorials, a docile promontory;
Who will erase the brisk clouds

Roaming the sky, in the chilly silence
Of night, like fire brittle harmattan forests?
Strangely fulfilling, like Leicester lifting the league cup.

The pendant hangs heavily on their hairy chests –
Crafted with chaff; a perfumed grave;
An outgrowth of rotted roots; apparitions appear

At street corners, stiff like stone, balking
The mist in the centre of River Forcados
The dead cannons, sunburnt, rising like a manatee

In the world of waters; trachea of bloodless tropes
Synthetic patrons of ailing roads, the filth festering
In white noses; the unwholesome stuff it infuses

In the blood traces its breath to flow stations
Lambent stuff in the klieg lights, a sullen poem
Written with water in the harmattan wind

Like a blinkered promise made outside the heart
Isolated from incandescent memory on dry sand dunes
Overarching the open sea, a dead stimulus

A stirring numbness, a mutilated bliss on the edge
Of ripening; the delta is drenched in dark dinosaurs
Of impalpable breed, like spirits, disbursing.

Lewd lessons; the desert is an active receptacle
Of liquid favours; a luscious lady lying like a lifeless log
In the company of opposite blood; the implacable

Blood in the inner being dissolves; a silhouette
Floats in ash or dying light, a blind route
To empty barns, always fresh, with some sort

Of eerily dark fragrance, like perfumed armpits
A suffocating bloom; a pig's delight
Is infinite in a wanton mixture

Of mud and water, a burst of beaming light
On the margins of being, announcing the death
Of the sky in turrets of strange gestures.

And a weft of vapour takes over the horizon
An alluring labyrinth; one smells some deviant fragrance
In the air again and again in this forest

Silence is grey in repressive climes; always
Ahead of a smelly opening of the mouth –
An outward growth of errant blood

Like carving a road on stone in a blind blaze;
A false promise, fleshy facades ride the wind
In starry essences; there is no assault

Or move, without some stubborn will
Winging in the deep, a restless mind
Moistening the margins of the soul.

THE BOUNDARY BETWEEN MAN AND SPIRIT

The windows are quirky wide open
To absorb the noon rays in their strides
The inmates pierce the bleeding light
Without bruises, to heal the wound

Of a hundred years, and the shadow;
The clamour for earthy cannons breeds
Untoward rehearsals in village groves.

The toddler smokes a rabbit dead in its hole
At Ogwashi-uku, opening up a road to his stomach;
The boundary between man and spirit
Is a road full of beacons, wholesome winds

Without salt or statistics
Peddlers of earthy gambits
In the grove full of eyes at night

A peculiar breed burrows in the wind
A shadow in flight, laden with crops
Imprinted on the howling horizon
Caressing the sea and stunted anthills.

One can pluck eggs from the sky
Without waking or straining
The world for a ladder –

The dream produces its own power
In the void, like Amassoma* Business centres,
Unblinking in session, making wanton meaning
Of the concept of self-government

---

* Hosts of the Niger Delta University, Bayelsa State, Nigeria.

Devoid of descants; setting pregnant sails
Against the tide, with no sweat springing
From combat or red secret distilled in shadows

No scar or promontory of combustious stuff
And it sets its own agenda
On the breasts of willowy winds and prayers
Powered by the caparisoned Orioke Babalola[*]

Empty of olive; waxing strong
Without fodder or antimony –
The world builds its treasures

On empty crab shells, on the seashore.
The entrails of the canticles
Laments of dancers, wearing white masks
Owners of the cinerary dumps

Littering the wind, leaning on perforated myth
Caught in their own nets
Strides made in snatches,

Like siesta among noisy children.
One needs discreet gestures in overcast skies –
Propitiation comes from white cobwebs
Muted airs, splintered green moments

Without vegetation, or heights close to heaven.
The broken barricades shone
With kernel oil in moonlight;

---

[*] Mountain of Babalola, Osun State.

No applause for the harmony of virgin blood
We abandoned at the crossroads
In the sky; the banal byways

Of vagabonds and songsters
Their endless musings, without moss
Or concrete anchorage; the streets
Teeming with ownerless skulls

From Boko Haram[+] bullets tucked
In sweet-smelling bouquets, or toddlers' tender pleas
The measured mendacities mowed down
In the middle of their flight to the moon,

Like the *akuu* tree;[*] solemn truths hidden in putrid waters
Of wayside gutters; risping winds carry no aplomb, the voice
    too
Gone awry with heated arguments in dishevelled
    bedchambers.

[+] A Jihadist group in Northeastern Nigeria.
[*] A kind of tropical tree, distinguished by its sturdiness.

IRON-MASKS

Iron-masks ride the highways of the world
Full of potholes and bumps; daylight funerals
Feed on birdsong, wakes to anthill –
The lurid burden of the soul

Long buried in tangled myths;
Let unquenchable flames of the earth
Devolve on the nakedness of blood-
A worn-out haven brooks no buffets or highlife

And the bubbling borders to a resurrection
In the air are constructed with coin;
Earthy wreaths flail in the rain
A jubilee without melody in the open arena.

They say, a monkey bridge offers solace in a void:
Let doubters of the promise sink in broken plumes
Of their own postulates; there is always
A gang of mosquitoes in the choir

Abusing the blood of believers, satiating,
Like wavelashes on a picknicker at Bar beach –
That is where true light evolves
Cleansing smudged streams in the spirit.

A floundering passion gathers nothing
In the wind; runs away in consummate horror,
Like Amassoma GSS[*] students from Indoukpala[+]
A vacuous soul cannot carry the cross through twilight,

[*] Government Secondary School.

[+] In those days, when the foreshore extended to a quarter of the present-day river, that is, before erosion ate into the town, even in the seventies, a group of women with one breast eerily long, appeared at intervals at Amassoma, walking down the lonely footpath, seemingly returning from their farms.

Crumbling in venal vibes, highways in the wild
Perfecters of lust, the incandescence overarching
All faiths, even in the green beginnings –
Such distillate of love and estrangement

In lonely streets, a crystal ingot hidden
In vague strides, loaded voids in the mind;
A shadow can show decorum in willowed company
Practising protocol with fire on her loins?

A drifting cavalry, in indeterminate recesses of the earth
Abettors of a carked plundering of bedsteads underground
A conjugal beatitude, resilient and manifest,
A bustling effluvium on clustering clouds

Dispelling the ruination rumour mongers peddle
The lethargy of dismantled gangsters and clinkers
Who pose in the chandelier as spirit tenders
In a morgue of tripes and slovenly cheer.

At dusk, the bubbling birdsong turns out a counterfeit
Masked in comic fissures and shadow
At the quadrangle besides the amphitheatre–
Mute conventions are always exploited in candid ways.

A FESTIVAL OF LONG SHADOWS

The despoiled world flows like virgin River Forcados
In the ultra-glow of her lover in the distant sky
Like the measured craft of a mythic master
Chiselling infinite moods in the blood, stroke by stroke,

Before the shadow of crude abscesses in a catacomb
Stole her virgin pride, ditching her dainty place
Amongst silver shingles on the shore
The inviolable sanctuary of mangrove splashes.

The waters weave thresholds of varied moulds
On a void canvas, scanty and shrivelled,
Into eternal voices of thunder, resonating
In open slums that bring out the mass of legends

Sheltering empires stripped
Of the soul of God; without
The town crier's gong, the cheering throng
Feeds fat on wind, insaned by the urge

Of naked blood, inheritors of the green space
Subliminal ghosts spangled on hefty farts
Buried in roving annals of the wind
Chain and dream are breathless allies on earth.

Hurray to the long shadows that salt festivals of life
Beguiling miracles that harry heartlands
The unseen war of beetles and termites
On the deep green of broken beginnings.

Holed drums provide soul stabbing music
Drunken tsetse flies dance in the open horizon
Phantom ships berth on the harbour of the mind
The crew so pale – no homely hues in hell

Underground outposts promote scurrilous prophecies
Scourge of benighted latchets; uncharted
Territories in a web in the rain
A beatitude so ruinous in its sparkle

The uncircumscribed vision of the hippo at night
Behind the downfall of the professed infallible,
Who see beyond the beyond, overturning
The boundless hand of providence.

AN AZURE FRAGRANCE

Thunder unreleased grows to a rock in silence;
Who would ignore a nocturnal mingling of blood in moondew?

An azure fragrance, as assured as a clipped cloth
In tropical winds; a marquee maker of marbled memory

A puddle of promise, a strange rainbow (without a sign of rain)
A morbid greenery breaks through synthetic clouds

Burns the soul of savages; seaweed
That sustains breath in ebb tide, in foul winds.

A cracked dream in delirious depths
Clears the ailments of blood buried in fine faces

Their antics subterranean and volcanic all at once;
A stellar speech riddled with crepuscular propositions

A burst of stony songs; patriots now congregate
With daggers and cudgels hidden in the choruses

Holding the lamp aloft which darkens
The breezy path to the sun, providing no foothole

A castaway, heaped out of green meadows; again and again,
This earth needs a mop, not an effete broom

Half human, half spirit, rummaging distant dumps
Drifting in the open sea; the whistle-blowing

In false winds, like a tailor toying
With a client's patience, in the imminence of Yuletide

A babel of excuses accentuates the inward fire
The fascinating rubble of the enemy camp

A maudlin illusion? Dark beyond dark
Roving within oneself; nowhere near

The cogent bridle of a born bard –
A captious breed making sport of conceited dross

The tangible spirit of a mutant meandering
Through smog and sparkle, swathed in slimy blood

Primed for a despoiled weather, devious bustle
Of senses; there is no monolithic lurid impulse

The rainbow is the lure; mournful and monumental
There is no jostling of the earth without blight

The gospel of the age takes the front seat
Glowering for a nose-dive, in the calculus

Of naysayers; a goal comes when the backline
Slightly goes to sleep, a lax latitude causes a drift

Even in sunrise; only death defeats time's impulse
A throbbing cemetery in the soul on high

When love withdraws fire from the hearth
A tangled openness weaves worms in the air

The poet slips out of home in the dead of night
To use made-in-Nigeria herbs in a London hospital;

Breeds strange nightmares; bonds which dilate the soul
In sullen defacement - dark tattoos assail the wind, awakening

Nipples long grown ash in the closet of memory
Midnight hurricanes test human blood in the middle of the
river

Swaying the syllable of stony dreams
Invincible in the unending myths of breath –

The unobtrusive throne of light; even mermaids
Regret the dance with humans in water;

A flawed consanguinity breeds fevered dreams
Floating in the head, like crude oil on water.

OPEN VOID

Toddlers open out to the infiniteness of blood
Counterpoise the downward spiral of dust
At twilight; uncontrollable lust on the corridors
Of harmattan winds; reeking revelries taken over
Street corners, deflect luminous hues of dawn;

No patriot overturns sanctions because they touch blood
relations –
Again and again, a goal comes when the backline
Slightly goes to sleep; something like an inebriated circus
To the die-hard fan – furiously jabs at his sanity;
The green herbage that heals the world

Could sprout from fractured roots, or rocky interspaces
A hardened soul needs moisture; some easement
To yield flowers of the heart, grow health
Dance in the sun without a mask;
Red blood craves some green cushion

Blood feeds on blood, to enliven wearied joints
Straighten out wrinkles, geriatric marks
Prime her pulse in searing cannonades, hoist
Savoury songs on hilltops; not the hard
And empty stuff in the air, like the shell

Of a clam; all fragments of fiery fuss
This river is motionless; sometimes, in stark regression
A mermaid sits at the centre of a maelstrom
Awaiting appeasement; green leaves flawed
By wanton caterpillars; leftovers manure the bare soil

Equipping the earth for man and beast
To pee on; an anchorless backward surge
Salving the secrets of dust; an ancient mantle
So closely guarded; like the bonding value of oil fish
Vague things sail on the sky-tide

Waiving the fog of brimless crowds
Anonymous; people without people
Ominously silent, or grumbling, or blatantly querulous
In the splintered streets, slashing blood
Which blossoms in crispy harpy hues

Recipients of lachrymal laurels that wake sleep
Or push life to a sleepless place
Sewn with sap in the wind, in water,
In shadows in drift in the open air
Isolated from fragrant groves in darkly blossom

A muted maniac is always in the spirit
Calculates new shortcuts to paradise; twisting
Destiny's hand, the abiding fart trailing
Childhood dreams, garlanded gems lying fallow
In the unnavigable depths of River Forcados

A dissolute bloom; pawns of superior blood
A surfeit of nauseous rites; undress the thunder
Whose echo petrifies a lion to the bones, running
To the nearest havens; the aching testament
Unfurls in a burst of brackish verse.

MASKED DANCERS FILL THE AIR

Painted patriots encircle the streets before dawn
Enchanting dancers, with fleshy hips
Avid archways registered in their blood
The sulphuric spark in their shiny eyes
A monument to the moss woven in their hearts
A lustreless lubberly hoax thrust in the air

Leaving their mass victims nude and lost
In a blaze of mental conundrum; a bruised song
In a welter of twisted words, or ghostly laughter
Slashing the throats of the gullible and greedy
Clustering clouds assail the head afterwards;
The only fortress an impervious latitude

A wizened mien; not given to intangible castles
In some distant haven, bubbling out
Of some motherly mermaid, or lisping shadow;
Imagination leads mavericks to underground morgues
Unassailable essences numbed in a shower
Of eternal lines, unflagging in their raw bluntness

Which clothes the festivity floating in the open air
With bone and ash and rock, throbbing seasons
In the awning blindness of a bat;
In the cordage of a ravaging curse,
A primed heritage rattles the luminous eyelashes
Of lightning, her turbid Siamese ally

The mesmerizing meshing made in the meadow
The rainy season is a curse to lowland dwellers
In tropical climes; the drowning power of high tide
Instigated by *Benikuru kuru*;[*] indubitable, sulphuric
In gesture; an implacable seven-headed spirit
Torments the sage who extracts trunks from a living elephant

---

[*] A water god

His maniacal stooge the yawning void
Created by cancer or earthquakes, beyond
The rubbles of riverside homes razed by a ring
Of short-changed arsonists insisting on ransom;
Or government agents, ostensibly, to displace
Perceived assailants of the sea's frothy bounties

The landlord is hysterical, frozen in the spirit
Gazes at the denuded stones, the menacing move
Perfected by bludgeoning blood and cymbal
In otherwise dormant dawns; tracks the cannonade
Of nondescript plumb in the sky, the footfalls
Forever chilling, empty of respite

An arduous fardel; a ritual fire stuck mumbling
In the blood, pustular and plain
In the haunches of moats, maracas and cathedrals
A well-trumpeted muteness in Daniel's den
A dream deserted at the crossroads rings no bell
Gnaws at the wind, sundering bridal entrails of the sea.

THE VOYAGE OF LIGHT

I
The gall of the silent sea, unleashed
unto itself, like a recoiling mamba at sundown

Prowling white light, improvident fossilization
of drifting dreams, in garrotting highways

The ripples swollen on a plundered landscape
Like water poured into a tattered basket

Ungathering plumes, even in harvest time
Farmers, frail and floundering, diss the weather

Nocturnal overlords revel in their slothful savviness
Frantic undercurrents in the manger, pricking

Indifferent winds; who wouldn't when the surrounding
Space is a suffocating knot riddled with flares?

The abstruse air that cracks the sun
In the scallop sky, furtive footholds, maimed eucalyptus

A prickly bloom in the peak period, an open-ended field
No one dares broadcasts; human blood is damn mutable

Like a chameleon, engrafting extant colours
In a multi-layered black shrub, a temporary anchor

Takes you inside a skyscraper on a swallow's wings
Wise men are stuck in the depths of heights,

Which is a sleek move –
Chops off fright with colourful red knives.

II
Recant the goal in the scars of the soul
A bottomless river, a maimed patrimony in ascent

Breacher of earth's promises, in dire and odd hours
A burst of the sultry sun squandered without introspection

On the corridors of love, promptly interred
In charred tombs, ratcheted puddles of stillness

Bidding farewell when the stage is only set
A stultifying memory of strifes without bullets

A brain revolution; the smoke swirling in the horizon
Is loaded with action words and dead songs

Where salt is the ultimate seasoning or scourge
A guided glory on earth needs no ceremony

Or rites or preening propaganda of politicians
Caught in their own nets in the lingering half-light.

DWELLERS OF THE EDGE

I
This receptacle of outstretched tales, bleeding
Sunbirds in flight; salutary souls stray

Facing the flare in the middle of River Forcados
This white light is impotent, cannot lift

The sore mood seated for ages on their faces
The mind where everything lays claim to the earth

Plays host to a fulsome fanfare, scarring,
Treasures hidden in crude testaments, twisting

The weather's countenance in a melee
Eyes do not see, a welter of wrecks

Sliding into glowing ash; their shabbiness
Bulging in the purified rhetoric where brown leaves

Lie in state; dark spirits always roam the earth
Breathing under her armpits; the incandescence

Seldom smiles on dwellers of the edge, a pubescent fire
Lost in transit, slated for shaming in the cathedral.

II
The true poet remains defiant on the power
of flowing streams over mythical stones and rocks

The crocodile cannot halt the bubble in the word
In the village playground, though insensate in fluvial spheres

This earth is long starved of penance and contrition
Like a shrivelling seaman's spouse at Ighorue St.*

The Stations of the Cross dishevels shenanigan souls
Ascending with their wares, in the marketplace

The green haunches of favoured children
Always brimming with sumptuous spoilers.

Kekefiyai⁺⁺ sours in the house
When lips are blistered by fever

Besotted with sea at eventide, bloomy fireflies
Desolate in the air; pawns of savages

On a godless altar; a sedulous sermon
To a tingling crush, who keys in to the whirlwind

They say, there is more aroma in a queenly gait
Than a perfect dance step, doubled in sunbeams

The lips unfold the indiscretion of the rock
Sniffing the air for money-eaters in the enemy's camp.

The lightning, a bottomless token of love and myth
Cringing shoulders crying wolf in a convent.

---

* Warri.
⁺⁺ A super delicacy of unripe plantain pottage in Bayelsa State.

STREET SONG

I
There is a melee in the hurrying streets
That carries the burden of charred roots
The company lithesome; yet stoking the dead moon!

Ever active sediments of the corals
of the beginning breed guttural outrage
In timed spots; burns the earth like live coal

Buried in the moon over the town hall
Assailed without cessation, by the surface smiles
Covering underground plots, enfolding the hardened blood

That rides the wind; the godly hinges
Of remembered festivities and deserted fishing camps
Famished sails and journeys ending in the beginning

The canoe and the voyage must speak
With one voice, that the looped puke
Of crossroads may crumble; that caged birds

May dream without thaws in the homestead
The underbelly the priest labours to unknot
Full of saucy entrails and black thread.

II
There is a garland of beacons in the streets
Striding into open doorways of stillness
Busy nudging on, or rather, unravelling

Broken spells too familiar and far-fetched
At once; even in their frothing anonymity, even
In the pits covered with fresh cocoyam leaves

The mildew medley of cloud and dung
Woven in sunlight, slips into streets
Of bridal trains and unfinishing intrigues

Man's bloodless self-arsenal splits sane airs
The anthem of antimony, though, hooded
is, itself, multi-layered; a miasma of sorts

Swathing hot veins, validating cosmic guilt
Coursing through cavernous nestlings on the peaks
Of deep green forests, breeding soaring edges.

THE ROAD TO HEAVEN

And the nebulous pews attract a swarm
Of white souls throbbing in their inner recesses
Like a strayed Jerusalem pilgrim; the road to heaven

Is long and dry, sometimes hanging
Like an overhead bridge paved with rotten plywood
Sometimes, hosting incandescent suitors – their origins

Prickingly unknown, feeding
On white myth, skewed desires, twisted
And tainted trances, carnal revelry in brothels;

The priest in search of swanky bullets and jeeps
Roaring across the six worlds of the earth, sinks
Deep into toothed dreams, like an eagle's talon

Engraved in a prey's crimson flesh in moonlight
And we are left with nothing, practically nothing,
After the priest has made his choice; left

With a tangled breeze lullabying us
Into acquiescence that the meat, primed
In the storehouse is the priest's to savour

And there is no argument beyond the crucifix
In the precincts of the cathedral
Where the white spirit lives beyond doomsday,

Beyond mortal drift, the ephemeral bubble
Of expansive seas, after the sun has gone to roost
Voiding the blood of harmony gurgling in the air

Like a thrifty landlord the tenancy of a lunatic
Countless slips lace the path of stone
Like morsels of *eba* transported by slippery okra

Down the throat, beyond the reach
Of rodents and prying spirits –
The sun mends the cracks of blood

Having no roots or mating-mates;
A burst of facades in fine apparel
Shying away from the pangs of penance.

How else does one pulverise and polish
The soul at once, treading light and wet wedges
When the river dwells in the canoe?

How else does one trigger the end
Of the internecine war in the blood
In the middle of day? A tender thorn

Is treacherous beyond damnation;
No matter what happens, the conqueror's house
Is full of fanfare; rustic mates

In high life with succulent nightbirds in homecoming
And living waters rush, above the revelry,
From the lane leading to the lair;

The haughty shade of whispering palms...
The cobweb spun in the languid air catches the spirit
Of man swollen in flight, otherwise invisible in light.

INCENSE

The sweltering priest in the offal
Wears a scented shine, swathing
Black raddles floating in the spirit –
Compost of aphrodisiacal incense.

The world enacts heresy
At the moment of reckoning
So pustulant they are better bridled at birth
The platters of music swollen with ritual

The illusory substances fostered by filth
Unconcealable counterfeits of all shades
Fused in abiding festivals in the wind
Moving from carpet to carpet in the name of God

Whinnying something about shadows and vampires
Deeper strife than the whirlpool at Ofonibengha* –
A born-again picks a brother's car key
With an inbuilt security apparatus

In a dream, promptly removes the censor,
Feigns ignorance when probed.
Cadavers and chimeras and lost souls
Tangible aloofness of catechists carked by conceit

On daily capital, fixed, like the time
On a spoilt wall clock at the cathedral
Patriarchs play pranks on the rainbow
In a crackle of subdued colours

_____

* A riverine community.

Mute and motionless, like a body guard;
Bereft of respite, like a gravedigger's impulse
A despoiled virgin incapable of utterance
Deepens the cut; the subtle swagger

Primed with the pith of plaudits in the wind
Breathed upon the ego; frail pieces
Which decompose before sundown
Leapfrog sensual borders and spasm

The swallows pointing the wrong way
In their bounteous cordage and nightairs
Sift the chaffs of patrimony in sky-gardens;
Solitude hobbles the soul, the unyielding

Monotony of black candlelights; laughing saints
Finger the planet with white gloves
Incandescent mourners dandle merry Christmas
Huddled in lent; ponderous wayfarers

Fondling the gates of hell, intoning hosanna
On the silvery eyelashes of mermaids
The slothful salacities, like unhealable blizzards
Which undress the moon in her full bloom

The shrine wetter than an extant well
The brain primes its petals in the troughs
Pummels pathways through mundane mires
The infinitude of God howls in the air.

SOFT STONES

Spewing healthful brine and booze
On a welter of soft stones and ash
Luminous waters go down the stream
In the throbbing silence of a sober bard.

Who would descant daylight cramps
Oiled by silky motes in the mind?

One hardly thinks argumentators will make heaven
Assailing the still air of graveyards
Where heaven-bound ghosts do dress rehearsals
With ever-fading footfalls in a burst of leavings.

Mundane essences, long marooned on tangled,
Sweet-smelling flowers, harbour shrines
Abandoned to cobwebs and thistle
To sooth tastebuds in an open brothel.

A race of white blood, awaiting doomsday
In patches the world soon forgets;
The dryless whirlwind in a tortoise's head
Shows the way inveterate rivers flow.

Now penance lives in buffets and coups
Loaded, variegated, blazing, in the nipples;
Wrinkles are adornments of God
To mark the years of debauchery since the first creation

Cormorants of moving moons; the sober essence
Stalking the pubescence of night minstrels
Who dispel lustreless latchets
Glazed in gruelling sunlight and lyre.

A pilgrimage is a dream of ascent
Hollow on the hinges, without the Godhead
Burnished sedulous on the loins
Like eventide caught on camera.

Wear the swankiest cassock on the cathedral
On the riverside; triple the tithe at Uselu[*]
Culled from the streaming offertory of congregants
Where cherubs frolic in the frozen weft

Of unseen casinos; a nondescript blossom
In brackish waters where pilgrims scatter
Like scared ants for self-succour –
The first law on earth

Each hewing its own rock
In feverish shores; crumbling ministrants
Of stagnant waters – a muted
Peripatetic cloud tans the dew-draped void

That routinely leads homeward in unbroken strides
The funerary gestures of the owl
Strewn on the archway, putrescent
In their skeletal imaginations, strips

The distances of self-distilling phobia
Crossing the boundary of doubt
Evident in one ounce of blood;
An abundance of intangible entrails

---

[*]In Benin-City, Edo State, Nigeria. A pastor of one of the prominent Pentecostal churches purportedly vowed to triple his tithe, in the wake of the controversy that Christian tithing generated.

Marks the gods' yawning disbelief
An abundance of sun and cymbal
As mutual fodder, like bridal gifts;
The bleeding light on the cross

Full of sapling and dross
Breaks the riddle of crumbling weather
Clears the cobwebs of failings
prompted by enchanted promises

In synthetic twilights; black seeds
Scoff at slick farmlands grandma
Cleared with cascading sweat and grit
Muffling the tingling song at birth

The clotting of recondite marmalade in the cathedral
On the sense's highway sunders motes sprinkled with ash;
A blossoming spendthrift in a cannonade
Of charred hymns, swollen alleyways and fruitage.

CARNAL MOONS

Fleshy fruitage sprouts from the crucifix,
Opens up to the vapours in the sky
Showers of light and green leaves
In tickling monody, along deserted shores.

A skeined triumph, heaving in birdsong
The willowing wedge serves as ready consort
Down the sacred grove of *Asiyai bou*[*]
The power of the sun recedes in seedy arguments

Near the altar, couched in white catacombs
Seaming laughters that do not reach the stomach;
A regal moon, in full regalia, smart on the throne
Hides the sewage nattering on earth's lap

Hides sulky souls full of white foam
Dissolving into scorching beach sand;
Crystalline and dense and dainty
In the encircling nakedness, variegated

Witnesses to the uncircumcised gestures across the ages.
The clotted motions of man unlock the gate
Unto ever-smoky harbours, after a sizzling sea ride;
Such uneasy sweetness, like lemonade,

The crushing essence of carnal moons
That misled the hen into endless awakening
Precipitate plunges into brackish waters
Humongous stumps hidden in their bellies;

---

[*] A mystical forest.

The steepy whirlpool leads
To the starting-point of the road to heaven
Like a satiated whore, trapping the roving spirit
In the middle of the congregation

The eerie silence of the sea
Doubly cascading in the seasoned arguments
Over prices in the marketplace
The pressurizing pulse on shuttered hearts

In open hideouts, sensuous masterpieces
That scatter love and legends in the wind
The siege of mermaids and swirling waves
Gathering the world on their palms;

The hideous mask flailing in the horizon
Deletes primal pampers, pricks margin-dwellers
The infinite festivities on earth, accompanying
The miracles of the wind, without mementoes.

The beginning is always a countdown
To another conundrum in the countless facades
On feminine loins each moment enacts;
The snail meets its nemesis in a nightly meal of crabs.

UNHEARD DRUMBEATS IN THE AIR

A gush of bottomless awning prods the world
To a stir, like a shushing gesture to lonely souls.

A midday fart in the marketplace
Is the trademark of inveterate guts

The luminosity of a blind sage's lessons
In sacred foibles quoted in the wind.

Who can stop the coronation of blood
The ripening process of pomegranate, without cannons?

Who can prune early morning dews
On the green face of the withering earth?

Such squib of daring on God's throbbing beacons
Tests nature's openness and magnanimous cheer

Kneading harmonies with a fowl's feet;
Its yoke can colour the wind in the marketplace

Its path borderless with imperial pavements
Like inchoate birds on tree tops

In a sinking metropolis, ravishing
Unadulterated winds and the sun.

Open your eyes a little further;
There are myriad myths in a broken bouquet

A recurring mire in a soulful tickle -
Bristling epithets paint the vain man's dreams.

A radiant gift in muddy waters breeds shadows
Ruins the sun's yolky path behind sacred bulrushes.

EARTHY FOIBLES

I
The colour blaze of the monarch butterfly
Cuts through synthetic fogs; cartographing
The grey luminosity of things remembered.

A glowing plague builds a house in the horizon
Like tilapia bone hanging on a neighbour's throat
The enlivening early morning pepper soup turns tremulous

The thistled hearth beneath the cadences
Of a catechist's crushing waist freed
Along the passage way, in outstretched vows

The buoyant shadows pulling down
The latitude of a swallow in flight, seedy underwears,
Prodded stillness, without a season of harvests,

Bubbling scalds, pruned wellsprings,
Eternal turrets of torture floating
In the abiding radiance of spumy seas

The edgy contraction of wave-besieged shores
The unseen steeps of gently flowing streams
The disquieting cold wars over mundane mines...

Let old mindsets go with the ebb tide –
Self-effacing and coy – new mufflers and stickers
Replace the acidulous fruitage flying in ornate symmetry,

Like jubilant pigeons in the sky
Rooted in fables of tortoises and hyenas
Decanting fossilized feathers hoisted in myths

Or hauled at the white spirit at the door
Fuelling cosmic angst – thunder bids its time
In the grip of false hoofs

Startles the wayfarer in enchanted forests
Talking to leaves, mumbling dusty memories
Suckling primal pulses, at counterpoise

In steepy runways; the unanimity of foundering breath
Mingling with the mist in the air
The prompt trail of fireflies at ease

In the throbbing whirlwind, like *Olorogun*,[*]
Ears nailed to *Aworowo*'s[**] talking drum
The esoteric theatrics of the rampaging shark

II

An alluring onyx in painted rainbows
Riding the shadows set on delightful bougainvillea;
Splintered marbles are incapable of airs
Dehydrated sparrows flutter in chattering forests

Crowned with long speeches that unearth
Fragrances buried in shallow depths
In the encircling bulrushes
In the alluring moonlight

The sprinkling songs that screen the sapphire
In open smog, moistened monocles,
Synthetic smiles in rarefied harbours
The leafless foliage notched to the wind

---

[*] Biggest masquerade in the Ayakoromo annual masquerade festival.
[**] Master drummer.

Dreams of green breath; sable horsemen of kindred thresholds
Always recede in pubescent streaks of light
Probing night markets, with career merchants
In cloying sprinkles of dewdrops

Bragging about yolks, in grey tunnels...
But, on land, are hippos not vulnerable,
Calcifying mortal blood in fluvial spheres?
Fair maidens unleash invisible spells

Cast in innocuous mouths and gestures
Which bound and rebound in space
Making rivers to miss their courses -
Taking a detour to unknown destinations

Like adventurous children's catapults the agama lizard,
On uncompleted buildings on the island of no regrets
And at eventide, one beautiful day,
I saw, through the window, seven black birds

Perch on a small forest behind my lowly home
Some young men ran to the spot, in curiosity.
In a flash, I saw a python as long as
Seven stretchered men on their shoulders

The world suffers irretrievable stasis
A conquered sphere in the frenzy
Of a forsaken spirit – the cowed sun
Scampers for breath, abandoning sky and blood

When dark clouds are fast asleep – chased
By a roaring army without a name;
Without pulling a trigger; some cubicles
Are too heated up for habitation,

Even in the harmattan season
Without a conflagration the eyes can see
Skin-deep volcanoes erupt from the abyss
Of the dishevelling sobs of a jilted heart.

The dinosaurs are always at merry,
Though furtively, their farms
Do not diminish; their clones on stage
Beget treasures with prevarication

Dinosaurs who entranced us with dance steps
And cavernous nestling –
Temperance left our shores for eternity
Since the first birth ended in heated arguments.

CASCADES OF MEMORY

Swift swallows end up in air-traps
Harlequins in mournful catacombs in the midday sun
A foul underbrush, steep watermarks...

Oddly long logs lie across
The road to light, beyond *Eyoro**
The flowery unction profaned

In beer parlour conversations.
The keyword to the stars is intangible
Wayward in its mode of intervention, though

Resplendent among furrows hewn from briny melody
In drilled domains and awning; stunting
The stakes in the sky, heard in the spirit only

Without the paleness of malarial pressure
Of sultry suns on callow limbs
Of fragile dinosaurs with hoary slogans

Of the harmony between the cat and rat.
The tarmac of a tumultuous trajectory
The jocund cascades of memory

Awake in a niggling void, or in ever approaching footfalls,
In the middle of night, a voyage of white-bearded clouds
Gripping fanfares, straining in a greenhouse

Despoiling the open fields of unclotted blood
Those buntings without weight or size
High waves in the mind of an upstart

---

* A village seer.

An alluring incandescence tanned with dross
Where light leads the funerary dance
The accursed sandbank gives way

To an amorous stillness, on time's lap
The untameable mule carries the terrestrial burden
Of labyrinthine laughters, on engrossing river baths

Where one inherits the wayfarer's excrement and oversight;
The unquenchable quest for naked interspaces
Shakes the myth of lightning down to the roots

Without any form of oblation, inscribed
In synthetic sanctuaries, without hired choristers
Or rabble rousers, routine stiflers of the harpy course.

The hype is ruined in the sauce
Sulking the albumen in the pantry
With mundane sacrifices, a prayer of deliverance

Hangs midair, like broken javelins
The value lost before the measured landing,
Like the splintered apocalyptic wings of Ejigbo.[*]

---

* On the 26th of September, 1992, a Nigerian Air Force plane crashed in the Ejigbo canal, Lagos, Nigeria, Killing all 158 people on board, including 8 foreign nationals.

PAINTED HARMONIES

Suffused in the gathering harmonies
Of desperate flutes blown
By despoilers of early morning
Drizzles in drowsy bedsteads

Smothered strides in resplendent rays
Paved with red myth; crowded with crosses
The inconsistent seascapes in sibylline light –
Tunnels endure an adamant memory.

The identity of estranged bonds,
Languid and laborious, in sunny forests –
Who begs for a disclaimer in absent crowds?
Surrealist dishes served in clay bowls

Pointed nipples are somnolent bullets
A nameless trench, a timeless facade
A delectable sin man enjoys on a platter
Of palm wine, signalling a homecoming

Untrackable footmarks of an antagonist
Clothed in the green of the forest
Lordly folks going after painted angels
Fatuous, one-side acquaintances, full of worm

The quintessence of a defiled bud
Laid as wreath, to mark a memory
A pusillanimous enterprise, deliberately skewed
A harrowing foliage, showing traits of self-abnegation

The secret bubble of man-made missions,
Shadowy and lonely, without heartbeats
Untrumpeted, without the tingling touch of dew
A menacing fecundity on desecrated seas

A yawning vacuum full of waves and bile
Plunging the earth into irretrievable crosscurrents
With the pensive trickle of lust and laughter
On abstinent loins; the pulse of fluvial festivities

Descanting the godhead, smashed to smithereens, in half-light;
Withered songs sound well on glorious lips.
A maul flowers in secret, though without chlorophyll
An arid sunburst, full of fantasy

A demobilized monster, a sodden owl overnight
Spewing malcontentment, on the hinges of a rock
Where power shows its bloodless claws
In cascades, aligned to the incandescent moon

Whittling down salted winds, wraithful gendarmes
On the prowl; unimpeachable voices
Trenching the throne, threshing transcendental shrines
On the solitary pathway to the riverside

The incestuous shadow, honed in strife
The discoverer of virgin tributaries
Receptacles closed and blazing in the closet
Scattered irretrievably in a playful subterfuge

Insatiable slippage in grilled clouds
Far, far away from expiration;
Who will purify the watery garbage
Fouling the luscious rhetoric of poetry

On the streets, in vain byways,
So-called social outlets, thriving
In ambiguity and negation,
Tracking the footfalls of the elephant

The burden of billowing fanfares
The predatory blood of freeways
And pulverized bile; gratuitous
And disconsolate, like simulated sex?

THERE IS PROMISE IN A PUDDLE

Resplendent dance steps from within
Spell raddles of conjugal bliss
Which resonate in the estrangement of the soul
Where the umbilical cord is buried

Such a mildew matrix of consanguinity
Empty bag carriers babbling propositions
Without yolk, scythed supplements
Oozing traits of a rotten tilapia head

Where threshers preach fat and flesh
In a puddle; there is no succour in sputnik
Flashes of stones, crystal of husks
No hive in a gratuitous warehouse

Anonymous litanies, familial salt
Evaporating in droves, in translucent configurations
In the bile of smoky shoals
Caught with dynamite and guile

In the solitary spine of twilight
A beautiful viscera of shadows
Walking on the shores, exuding
Metallic passions of women paddling away

To prized beginnings when they brooked
No flinches or passes or faces
Now buried in painted rock and stone
The smell of densely-populated convents

Transcendental in the evolving music
In the sky, the benign colouration
Of incest in cathedrals peeing on
Ancestral shrines laden with cobwebs

The bland ambiguities of a poetaster's art
Lisping the languid loopholes that last a lifetime;
Strangers complete a journey with manuals
Lacking the evergreen whims of aborigines

Silvery birdsongs in the meadow haunt
The dense, dreary clouds, numb to the lancet;
The vast expanse of white fields close to the riverbank
Owned by atonement, remains a virgin enclave.

YESTERDAY'S MIST

Sallow oysters decorate the foreshores of Burutu[*]
Prompting memory, foiling the flow of blood –
A quiet lust in the bustle of butterflies
Caressing coconut trees on the harbour.

The morbid purity of virginal senses
Distinct from wayfarers sleeping on godly altars
Malevolent claws caught piercing comets
Husks clogging flowing water

In homely frontiers, headlong in a goblet
Of growing greens; the spoiler of open doors
In fellowship with long drawn-out pagans
Who stalk the highest mountain in woodsmoke.

And here comes a colleague so drunk and late
In the night, a wheelbarrow carries
Him home; in that messed-up state
In the monotony of bland prophecies

My colleague talks of the naked prisms of the wind
Tumid haunches of dinosaurs who show the way
Through white light, to the lunatic's growth
In duel and grime, on effulgent archways

A fouled foliage in white hand gloves stabs the mind
The evolving dawns only exhale yesterday's mist
The glowing turbulence in bales of legit provender
Hurrying migrations across unalterable impulses

---

[*] A riverine community

Though unencumbered, impotent roots
Which need rinsing in the wind;
The quintessence of a blind dance
On a mountaintop

A revelling ascent to the stark bottom
Without a crash or sentient footfalls;
Starveling motes sentinelling the chasm,
To avoid convulsions, scarlet and raw

Enclosing the shared ruination of the soul
Infinite riversides, rustling honeycombs
Without cannons or gunpowder or snuffed water
Baring the early morning brigand and geraniums

Promptly teetering to the tortoise's funeral
In the pith of cathedral bells and homilies
The subterranean crisscrosses in the sea
Announcing new creeds,

Satiating as coconut water
In moon glow; the song on a sage's lips
Whispers a verity in the tortoise's repertoire
Where the river gives way to let a road pass.

A MORBID BEAUTY

"Too much book blinds the eye,
Like bile bars the tongue from fluvial flesh"
So persists my in-law and mentor
In a rare burst of wits, after
A gourd of off-whitish yester-up palm wine.

The howling numbs the conventional sense
Which, like parsley, needs sunlight and moisture;
The lubberly solicitude in recondite chains
Ending in illusions and allusions
Like unfurling flowers stunted in the sun

Leave vile memories, emblazoned
By the benevolent breath of a predator –
Countless trappings of bricks and bloodbath;
A goddess lies in tingling bedsteads in the waters
Basking in the separation from man hatched

In the heat of the moment, evolving
Into a saturnine serenity of both souls;
Do we talk of a plunge without conception
Or premeditation, which is a rational prerogative;
The protection of differing primordial milk?

The amethysts that crowd the city centres
Slithering down monuments; wrestling with waves
And intimate hinges on land, heaves
Up lodes of light in a dark tunnel,
Like the lion's limitless vision at night.

The black world is a fallen eagle
De-winged and without gauntlet
Groping in a monastical highway, the aurora teased
With open-ended knots, bearing stones and ash
Faltering and flailing in imaginary fever

Wings burdened by a wave of rubies
Need not stay, to stab the soul in loft
Transcending the haggardly indigent;
Let us measure the mutability of man
On the map of reticent skeletons

The muteness of niggling white pebbles
On the seashore, caressed by briny gusts of wind
In black gathering clouds in the diaspora
A signal of blazing whims sold to the ghosts
Who lead the rabble headlong, on long strides

Of brotherhood from the rear or reef;
The fugitive flashes his eyes, behind his hosts,
On scented sanctified hilltops, adorned
With dark wraiths and foam
 A flock of black birds in airy feast.

A cousin way back in Port Harcourt
In the early nineties, claimed to be a Captain
In the Nigerian army, mastering
The green airs and codes; Bori camp* opened
Her gates wide, with complimentary salutes to boot!

The ponderous man alters the flow of things,
In any form, without scabbards; no room
For wreaths stinking of dark incense
A Hippo's yawn is not fatigue;
Advertises its razor-sharp teeth.

---

* Nigeria Army, Port Harcourt.

TIMELESS MUSIC

These dangling shadows
Bearing secret grudges
In the midday sun

Braid the rough edges
Of penumbra blood
The moody miasma, into

Timeless music, ever playing
In the precincts of the mind,
Without prophecy or oblation,

Like a natural badge; a whiff
Of milky affirmation tied to the door
Of the cathedral in these dire times,

Surefooted, like an ancient blood knot
In dissonance with a cosmetic concert
Mounted by tiros who feed fat

On the blaze of klieg lights and billboards
Dissing the nocturnal treasures
Of moonlight tales!

Music interweaves coffins and Christmas
With a sumptuous abundance of palm wine
Beyond muffling or censor or iron claps

Beyond the frothing gaiety in ivory cups
Making final farewells a distant dream
Though tendered in loveliest courtesy

With the finest of faces; no make-up –
Resplendent voices reeling rainbow memories
Of sensuous sandbanks and sizzling sea breeze

Rooted in rustic palms of the beginning
Where stories of the tortoise and hyena decant
Fossilized blood hoisted in the wind

With effervescent precision and swagger;
Now black feathers are hauled at the spirit
Fuelling cosmic angst – music too

Can declaim the dictator sprinkled with ash;
Thunder bids its time on covetous palms
In the grip of false hoofs and hangovers.

Printed in the United States
By Bookmasters